KU-686-608

A GUIDE TO JEWISH KNOWLEDGE

A

A GUIDE TO

JEWISH

KNOWLEDGE

by

THE REV. DR. CHAIM PEARL
M.A., Ph.D.

and

THE REV. REUBEN S. BROOKES

with a Foreword by

RABBI DR. ISIDORE EPSTEIN
B.A., Ph.D., D.Litt.
Principal, Jews' College
London

LONDON
JEWISH CHRONICLE PUBLICATIONS

Jewish Chronicle Publications
37 Furnival Street
London, EC4

First Edition 1956
Second Edition (Revised) 1958
Third Edition 1961

Set in 11/12 Bembo by The Sharon Press, London,
and printed and bound in Great Britain by
Tonbridge Printers Ltd., Tonbridge, Kent

Foreword by

Rabbi Dr. ISIDORE EPSTEIN, B.A., Ph.D., D.Litt.
Principal, Jews' College, London

"A man should always teach his disciples in the shortest manner." This is the sound pedagogic principle, enunciated by the Talmud, which has been adopted by the Rev. Dr. Chaim Pearl and the Rev. Reuben S. Brookes, who are both well-experienced teachers of Judaism, in preparing this *Guide to Jewish Knowledge*. The aim the authors set themselves was to give the reader a knowledge of the essentials of Judaism, presented in the simplest possible manner, "so that he may run who readeth it."

The authors have accomplished their task with success. The information conveyed in the work, within its strictly circumscribed limits, is concise, accurate and to the point. The book should prove of value not only to beginners, but also to those who wish to refresh the knowledge they have imbibed in their early days, and moreover serve the reader as a spur to further study.

I have much pleasure in commending this work, which should appeal to a large circle of Jewish readers.

Introduction

The purpose of this book is defined by its title and it is hoped that it will appeal to laymen who seek knowledge about the basic beliefs and practices of Judaism.

Recognising the popular and utilitarian value of this little book the authors have aimed at the virtues of simplicity and clarity and have deliberately omitted anything that seemed to them too complicated or outside the strict boundary of a guidebook. At the same time they have been careful to include everything that is of fundamental importance. The book is clearly divided into convenient sections to facilitate quick reference and wherever possible the Hebrew terms, which are often the key words to the understanding of Jewish ideas, have been included.

In compiling the book the authors have had in mind the needs of youth and adult. In the classroom it can be used as a textbook while the adult may keep it as a handy reference book supplying him with information on all the main headings of Jewish knowledge. The last two sections on Jewish History and on an outline of basic Judaism have already been used very successfully by the authors with various groups and Synagogue circles where each chapter formed the basis for intelligent study and discussion.

Grateful acknowledgment is made to the Rev. Dr. A. Cohen, Mr. Harold Levy and Dr. Alex Tobias for their many useful suggestions and particularly to Rabbi Dr. I. Epstein for his numerous suggestions which have been incorporated in the book and for his kindness in writing the Foreword.

C.P.

R.S.B.

Publishers' Note

The Publishers wish to express their thanks to the Council of the Birmingham Hebrew Congregation who have associated themselves with the publication of this book, written by the Ministers of the Singers Hill Synagogue. The publication was a part of the Centenary celebrations of the Synagogue and the assistance of the Council has enabled a public far beyond the boundaries of Birmingham to benefit from a book of lasting value.

Contents

Jewish Religious Observances

General

The Basic Sources of Jewish Life and Thought

JEWISH RELIGIOUS OBSERVANCES

I

The Calendar

The Jewish Calendar is lunar in character since the months are reckoned according to the time it takes the moon to travel round the earth. Each month consists of either 29 or 30 days. Since the lunar year consists of approximately 354 days while a solar year (the time it takes the earth to make a complete circuit round the sun) consists of 365 days, some adjustment of the lunar year has to be made to the solar year. This is done every few years by inserting an extra month in the lunar calendar. This happens seven times in nineteen years. If this were not done the religious calendar would become moveable so that, for example, the Festival of Pesach, which should always occur in the spring (in the land of Israel) would occur earlier by eleven days each succeeding year until the Spring Festival would be kept in winter.

A year of 12 months is called שָׁנָה פְּשׁוּטָה (an ordinary year).

A year of 13 months is called שָׁנָה מְעוּבֶּרֶת (an intercalary or leap year).

In a cycle of 19 years, a leap year occurs on the 3rd, 6th, 8th, 11th, 14th, 17th and 19th years.

A useful Hebrew mnemonic is גּוּ חַ אֲ דְּ זַ ט

(Each Hebrew letter has its numerical value. See Hebrew table in Section 15).

The Important Dates of the Jewish Year

Nisan: (Mar.-Apr.):	14th	Fast of the Firstborn.
	15th	Commencement of the Pass-over—פֶּסַח (8 days).
	16th	Beginning of counting of the Omer.
Iyyar: (Apr.-May):	18th	33rd of the Omer—לַ"ג בָּעֹמֶר
Sivan: (May-June):	6th and 7th	Feast of Weeks—שָׁבֻעוֹת (2 days).

I

Tammuz: (June-July):	17th	Fast commemorating breach made in the wall of Jerusalem.
Av: (July-Aug.):	9th	Fast commemorating the (*a*) destruction of the First and Second Temples (586 B.C.E. and 70 C.E.) (*b*) fall of Bethar (135 C.E.)
Elul: (Aug.-Sept.):		The Shofar is blown daily on the weekdays of the month. During the last week of the month Penitential prayers—סְלִיחוֹת are recited
Tishri: (Sept.-Oct.):	1st and 2nd	New Year—רֹאשׁ הַשָּׁנָה (2 days)
	3rd	Fast of Gedaliah
	10th	Day of Atonement—יוֹם כִּפּוּר
	15th	Commencement of the Festival of Tabernacles—סֻכּוֹת (9 days)
Cheshvan: (Oct.-Nov.):		
Kislev: (Nov.-Dec.):	25th	Commencement of Chanukah —חֲנוּכָּה (8 days)
Tevet: (Dec.-Jan.):	10th	Fast day commemorating the commencement of Nebuchad-nezzar's siege of Jerusalem
Shevat: (Jan.-Feb.):	15th	New Year for Trees—ט"ו בִּשְׁבָט
Adar: (Feb.-Mar.):	13th	Fast of Esther
	14th	Purim—פּוּרִים
	15th	Shushan Purim

In a Leap Year an extra month is added and the thirteenth month is called **Adar Sheni** (The Second Adar).

Note: In the treatment of festivals and observances the Ashkenazi (German or East European) rites and usages are followed. Sephardim (Jews of Spanish and Portuguese origin) have slightly different usages.

II

The Sabbath

Note: Readers who find an unfamiliar Hebrew term in the text should consult SECTION 9, A CLASSIFIED TERMINOLOGY (page 36).

The Significance of the Sabbath: The name of the seventh day of the week is derived from the Hebrew שבת which means simply "to cease from work". But the Sabbath is not only a day of rest; it is a day of holiness when man can for a short while put off the cares and material pursuits of life and devote himself to the refreshment of the spirit and religious activity.

The Sabbath is therefore fully observed only when there is both physical rest and spiritual recreation. This two-fold significance of the Sabbath is emphasised in the Ten Commandments and in other parts of the Bible also, where both the social and the religious aspects of the Sabbath are made clear. In the Kiddush, the social importance of the day is found expressed by the phrase—

זֵכֶר לִיצִיאַת מִצְרָיִם "A memorial of the departure from Egypt" when Israel was redeemed from physical slavery. Its religious significance is pointed to by the designation of the day as—

זִכָּרוֹן לְמַעֲשֵׂה בְרֵאשִׁית "A memorial of the Creation" of the Universe by God who is the creative power behind all that exists.

A Day of Rest: Prohibition of Work: Cessation from work is the first essential for the observance of the Sabbath. The rabbis defined "work" under thirty-nine chief headings which virtually embrace every kind of activity which is likely to break the sanctified rest of the Sabbath day. Tasks which seem to be similar to any of the thirty-nine main divisions of work were all prohibited, as well as many types of activity which would detract from the holiness of the Sabbath or which were regarded as too strenuous for a day of rest. In addition to these latter which are classified under the term שְׁבוּת (a term which refers to any act prohibited by rabbinic law on account of the sanctity of the day of rest) we also include the injunction against the enjoyment by a Jew of work done by a non-Jew. Rabbinic law also prohibits the handling of any object which may not be used on the Sabbath, since it would tend to make one forget the holiness of the day. This class

3

of prohibition is known as מוּקְצָה. In all cases of emergency, however, when there is danger to life, Jewish law requires that the Sabbath be broken to rescue life.

Observance in the Synagogue:

(*a*)   The services on Sabbath are different from those of the week. Friday evening service is called קַבָּלַת שַׁבָּת (S.P.B. 108a*) "The Inauguration of the Sabbath" and includes the recital of six nature psalms (95-99, 24) corresponding in number to the six days of the creation and the special psalm of the Sabbath (Psalm 92).

(*b*)   A central part of the Friday evening service is the famous sixteenth-century hymn composed by Solomon Alkabetz of Safed, known by its opening words לְכָה דוֹדִי "Come my friend to meet the bride." The Sabbath is poetically described in Jewish literature as the "Sabbath Bride".

(*c*)   Kiddush is recited in the synagogue towards the end of the service since formerly it was the custom to entertain wayfarers in the synagogue and the public recital of Kiddush would exempt them from reciting it individually.

(*d*)   The service in the morning has characteristic features of its own of which the most important is קְרִיאַת הַתּוֹרָה (Reading of the Law). It is generally assumed that public reading of the Scriptures goes back to ancient days, even long before Ezra (5th century B.C.E.) instituted more regular readings from the Torah. In subsequent centuries the Palestinian custom of reading through the Torah scroll every three years was replaced by the annual cycle in practice in Babylon.

The entire Pentateuch is divided into 54 weekly portions and the scroll is thus completed in the course of a year. Seven men are called to the reading of the Law and with the last person who is called for the reading of the מַפְטִיר (concluding paragraph) this is the largest statutory number of people called up in the synagogue on any sacred day.

After the סִדְרָא (portion from the Pentateuch) is read, the הַפְטָרָה or lesson from the Prophets forms an appropriate conclusion to the Scriptural readings. There are several suggestions as to the origin of the הַפְטָרָה. The most popular belief however is that the custom of reading the הַפְטָרָה commenced during the 2nd century B.C.E.

* S.P.B.—Singer's Prayer Book.

when the reading of the Law was prohibited by the Syrian-Greeks during the Maccabean struggles. Since the Jews would not read a portion of their sacred Five Books by heart, for fear of mistake, they resorted to proclaiming a portion from the latter books of the Bible which had some connection in subject matter to the weekly reading.

(e) After the morning service on Sabbaths and festivals an additional service is read. This is because while on ordinary days in the Temple two sacrifices were offered up, one in the morning and the second in the afternoon, on Holy Days additional sacrifices were made after the normal morning offerings. Since the order of the statutory prayers follows the order of worship in the Temple an additional service corresponding to the additional sacrifice was introduced on Sabbaths and festivals. This additional service (S.P.B. 159-166) is called Musaph (מוּסָף) from a Hebrew root meaning "to add" and comprises the first and last paragraphs of the Amidah and appropriate Scriptural passages relating to the additional Temple sacrifices on the sacred day.

Observance in the Home: It is chiefly in the home circle that the Sabbath is seen with all its great power of transforming drab workaday life into a joyous and spiritual experience. Preparations are made a day before in honour of the Sabbath. Friday is called עֶרֶב שַׁבָּת "Sabbath eve." The table represents an altar the sanctity of which is heightened by the loaves of bread, lighted candles and Kiddush wine.

(a) חַלּוֹת Two loaves of bread represent the double portion of manna which fell for the Israelites on Fridays during their travels in the Wilderness so that they did not need to collect it on the sacred Sabbath. The loaves are covered with a cloth symbolising the protective cover of dew over the manna.

(b) **Sabbath Lights:** Two is the minimum number, symbolic of the twin commands to "Remember" and to "Observe" the Sabbath; זָכוֹר, שָׁמוֹר (Exodus 20: Deut. 5, 12).

(c) **Blessing the Children:** (See S.P.B. p. 122c). On Sabbath eve the father places his hands on the heads of his children and utters a traditional blessing together with the prayer that they grow up after the pattern of the fathers and mothers of Israel.

Already in Bible times we find that a father's blessing was regarded of great importance. Throughout the ages it has come to symbolise the

5

joining of one generation to the next in a bond of mutual affection and loyalty to the Faith of Israel.

(d) קִדּוּשׁ   Kiddush is recited before the commencement of the meal. Wine is the symbol of blessing and joy; consequently it is usual to pronounce the Sabbath benediction with wine. If wine is not available the ceremony may be performed with the loaves of bread (S.P.B. p. 124).

(e) זְמִירוֹת   **Table Hymns:** Sabbath table hymns are sung during the meal. Most of the hymns speak of the gift of the Sabbath as the greatest religious treasure of Israel and the spiritual reward of those who faithfully observe the holy day.

(f) שָׁלֹשׁ סְעוּדוֹת   **Three Meals:** Three formal meals are prescribed for the Sabbath. The term, however is often used exclusively for the last meal on Sabbath afternoon which is often made elaborate by more זְמִירוֹת and religious discussion. The proper term is סְעוּדָה שְׁלִישִׁית "The Third Meal."

(g) עֹנֶג שַׁבָּת   **Sabbath Delight:** This is a term which has become popular in recent years and describes a Sabbath afternoon gathering for study, refreshment and social recreation. The custom was made popular by the poet Bialik in Eretz Yisrael and has since spread throughout the Diaspora.

(h) הַבְדָּלָה   **Farewell ceremony:** As it was welcomed with religious ceremony, so at the time of its departure the Sabbath is bidden farewell with religious ceremony. The word הַבְדָּלָה means literally "division" and applies to the colourful ritual performed with wine or other beverage (not water), lighted taper and spice box. The wine is made to overflow the cup and is an indication of the hope that the forthcoming week be everful with Divine blessings. The light represents the first product of God's creation and since the first act after the Sabbath is usually to put on the lights, the lighted taper has a fitting place in the ceremony which marks the beginning of a new working week. The blessing recited over the light refers to God the Creator of lights, and the candle used in the ceremony consists of several strands of tapers twisted together. The spices are used to remind us of the fragrance of the "added Sabbath soul" which has now departed. (S.P.B. p. 216).

6

III

Festivals

The Three Pilgrim Festivals

The Bible states, "Three times a year thou shalt keep a feast unto me." (Exod. 23, 14). This refers to the three joyful festivals in the Jewish Calendar, Pesach, Shavuot, Sukkot, known collectively as שָׁלֹשׁ רְגָלִים "The Three Pilgrim Festivals" since the Jews were commanded to make a pilgrimage to the Temple in Jerusalem as part of the celebration of these festivals.

Their chief importance is in their designation as festivals which commemorate three important stages in the history of the Israelites:

Pesach   —the Exodus from Egypt.
Shavuot   —the Giving of the Torah.
Sukkot   —the Journey in the Desert en route to the Promised Land.

These Pilgrim Festivals had also an agricultural significance:

Pesach   —Barley harvest.
Shavuot   —Wheat harvest.
Sukkot   —Ingathering of the produce.

a. Pesach (Passover)   פֶּסַח

1. **Purpose:** The Festival of Pesach commemorates the deliverance from Egyptian bondage and with it the birth of the Hebrew nation. It is the Festival of Spring (חַג הָאָבִיב) when nature comes to life again after the dark winter.

2. **Date:** Pesach is kept for eight days (seven days in Israel) from the 15th Nisan. The four middle days are semi-holydays known as חֹל הַמּוֹעֵד (weekdays of the Festival).

3. **Names:**

   (a)   חַג הַמַּצּוֹת   Festival of the Matzot, because of the commandment to eat מַצָּה "unleavened bread" and the prohibition against חָמֵץ "leavened bread" (Ex. 12, 15). This

7

is in commemoration of the hasty Exodus from Egypt when the Israelites had time to prepare only unleavened bread.

(b) פֶּסַח (i) The word means "to pass over" and is related to the passing of the Angel of Death over the homes of the Israelites to slay the Egyptian firstborn (Exod. 12, 27).

(ii) The Festival of the Paschal lamb and its sacrifice (Exod. 12, 3-20).

(c) זְמַן חֵרוּתֵנוּ Season of our Freedom; so described because it marks the liberation of Israel from Egypt and its birth as a free nation.

(d) חַג הָאָבִיב The Spring Festival.

4. Observances:

(a) **The Fast of the Firstborn:** On the day before Pesach, the 14th of Nisan, it is necessary for firstborn sons to fast. Called תַּעֲנִית בְּכוֹרִים this fast commemorates the deliverance of the firstborn Israelites in Egypt (Exod. 12, 23-4). It is usual for the firstborn to attend a Siyyum, a completion of a section of the Talmud, at which they partake of refreshments. They are then exempt from this minor fast.

(b) **The Search for Chametz:** On the eve of the 14th day a search is made for leaven throughout the home. This is called בְּדִיקַת חָמֵץ. After the search the leaven is set aside to be burned on the following morning. It is customary to place a few pieces of bread in various parts of the house so that the search be not in vain. It is, however, not right to collect only these pieces without making a search throughout the home. For full details of the searching and burning of the chametz see the Passover Haggadah.

(c) **Selling of Chametz:** Leavened commodities which cannot be disposed of before the Festival and are intended for use after the Festival are sold to a non-Jew so that any chametz found in a Jewish household is, properly speaking, not in the possession of the Jew. This procedure is very common in orthodox communities and is usually carried out by a rabbi on behalf of the seller. After the Festival the chametz reverts to the ownership of the Jew in accordance with certain prescribed legal procedure.

5. The Prayer for Dew: Besides the usual Festival service a special prayer for "dew" is recited on the first day of the Festival during the Musaph (additional) service. This prayer was composed by the medieval poet and liturgist, Eliezer Kalir (c. 670 C.E.) and is a beautiful petition for the blessing of abundant dew for the fields of the Holy Land.

6. The Seder:

(*a*) **Meaning:** The service celebrated in the home on the first two nights of Passover is called "Seder" (order). The service is divided into some fifteen sections each indicated by a descriptive name.

(*b*) **Purpose:** Its purpose is to symbolise important features and lessons of the Exodus and the redemption.

(*c*) **The Haggadah—The Narrative:** The Bible enjoins us to relate the history of Exodus to our children. Hence the Hebrew term "Haggadah" (narrative) which is the name given to the special book containing the order of service used at the Seder.

(*d*) **The Seder Dish:** The Seder dish comprises the following:

(i) **The Egg:** A hard boiled egg slightly roasted placed on the left of the dish representing the special festal sacrifice offered on the 14th Nisan in Temple times in conjunction with the Paschal sacrifice.

(ii) **The Shankbone:** A roasted bone placed on the right of the dish symbolising the Paschal lamb.

(iii) **The Bitter Herbs:** Some horse-radish symbolising the bitterness of the Egyptian bondage.

This is placed in the centre of the dish. In the Talmud it is suggested that lettuce be used for the bitter herb since it tastes sweet at first and then bitter. Likewise the Egyptians first honoured the Israelites and then persecuted them (Talmud Pes. 39a).

(iv) **Charoset:** This is a compound of apples, nuts, cinnamon and wine which popularly represents the mixture of mortar used by the Israelite slaves in their labours.

(v) **The Vegetable:** (Karpass). Usually parsley, which is dipped into salt water and eaten. According to the Talmud this custom was instituted to excite the interest of the children. A further reason given is that on the Seder night all are in the category of nobility who partake of an hors d'oeuvres before a meal.

(vi) **The Salt Water:** A dish of salt water is used into which the vegetable is dipped. It is suggested that the salt water represents the tears shed by the Israelites in Egypt.

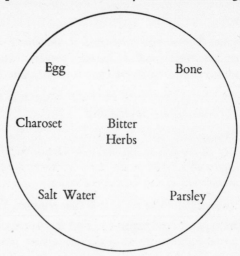

Egg   Bone

Charoset   Bitter Herbs

Salt Water   Parsley

(vii) **The Three Matzot:** Besides the above symbols three matzot are placed before the head of the family. Two of the matzot take the place of the usual two loaves of bread used at the Sabbath meal and the third matza is for the purpose of making a special blessing for the ritual eating of matzot. It has been suggested in addition, that the three matzot point to the three sections of the Jewish people—Priests, Levites and Israelites.

(viii) **The Four Cups of Wine:** These are drunk in token of the four expressions of redemption mentioned in the Bible (Exod. 6, 6-7).

וְהוֹצֵאתִי	"And I shall bring out."
וְהִצַּלְתִּי	"And I shall deliver."
וְגָאַלְתִּי	"And I shall redeem."
וְלָקַחְתִּי	"And I shall take."

(ix) **The Cup of Elijah:** There was some doubt if a fifth
Biblical expression of redemption וְהֵבֵאתִי "And I shall
bring" should also be symbolised making it necessary for
five cups to be drunk. It was therefore decided to have the
extra cup and entitle it "the cup of Elijah" since all unsolved
problems in the Talmud await the decision of Elijah.
During the service the door is opened for the arrival of
Elijah. At one time it was usual to leave the door open
throughout the Seder as an invitation to strangers to enter
and participate in the Seder. In the Middle Ages when
Jews sometimes had to keep the Seder in secret because
they feared the possibility of attack, this practice was
abandoned and instead, the door was opened for a moment
in symbolic welcome of the Prophet. The figure of Elijah
is especially appropriate for Passover since in Jewish
tradition he is the herald of the Messiah and therefore
points to a future period of perfect freedom and peace.

(x) **Afikoman:** אֲפִיקוֹמָן a word derived from the Greek
meaning "dessert". This refers
to the final piece of matza eaten at the end of the Seder
meal and symbolises the last meal (the Paschal lamb) the
Israelites ate in haste prior to the Exodus. There is a custom
to hide the Afikoman allowing children to find it and earn
a reward for doing so. This is simply an additional
incentive to the children to maintain their interest
throughout the Seder. One notices that the whole Seder
service has been arranged for the children since the rabbis
deduced from the Biblical instruction וְהִגַּדְתָּ לְבִנְךָ ("And
thou shalt tell it to thy children") that the children are to be
instructed on the significance of the Festival.

(xi) **The Counting of the Omer:** The 49 days separating
Pesach and the next Pilgrim Festival, Shavuot, are counted
day by day. This counting begins on the second night of
Pesach (Cf. Section 5c).

b. Shavuot (Pentecost or Feast of Weeks) שָׁבֻעוֹת

1. Purpose: This Festival is observed to commemorate the time when the Children of Israel received the Law on Mount Sinai. Its agricultural significance is that it marked the beginning of the summer harvest in ancient Palestine.

2. Date: The 6th and 7th of Sivan (one day in Israel).

3. Names:

(a) חַג שָׁבֻעוֹת

The Feast of Weeks (Exod. 34, 22). So called because a period of seven weeks is counted from Pesach to this Festival. This period is called "The Counting of the Omer" from the original law governing the offering of an Omer (measure) of barley from the new produce.

(b) זְמַן מַתַּן תּוֹרָתֵנוּ

The Season of the Giving of the Torah. It is so called because seven weeks after the Exodus, the Israelites assembled at the foot of Mount Sinai when the Ten Commandments were proclaimed by God.

(c) יוֹם הַבִּכּוּרִים

The Festival of the First Fruits (Num. 28, 26). Since it is the summer Festival corresponding with the beginning of the harvest the Jews joyously brought an offering of the best ripe produce of the fields as a thanksgiving to God.

(d) חַג הַקָּצִיר

The Feast of the Harvest (Exod. 23, 16). So called to indicate that it was the season of the wheat harvest.

(e) עֲצֶרֶת

Concluding Festival. Known by this name since it is the "Concluding Festival" to the Passover. Another reason for this name is that Shavuot has no major symbols or distinctive rites and its single festival feature is the prohibition of work עָצוּר מִמְּלָאכָה.

4. Observances: In its observances both aspects of the Festival—the historical and the agricultural are portrayed.

(*a*) **In the Synagogue:** The Ten Commandments are read in the synagogue on the first day.

(*b*) The Bimah and the Ark are decorated with flowers to symbolise the slopes of Sinai which were covered with vegetation.

(*c*) The pious stay up the whole of the first night of the Festival and study an anthology of sacred writings called

תִּקּוּן לֵיל שָׁבֻעוֹת—A Shavuot night Lectionary.

(*d*) The Book of Ruth is read for its delightful background of a summer harvest and also because King David, who was a descendant of Ruth, was born and died on Shavuot.

(*e*) In some congregations it is usual to read a liturgical poem entitled אַקְדָּמוּת before the reading of the Law on the first day. This poem is ascribed to Rabbi Meir b. Isaac of Orleans (11th century). It eulogises the Jewish people and their love of God and His Law.

(*f*) **Home Customs:** Milk dishes are the customary foods, symbolising the Torah which is likened to milk for its nourishment.

c. Sukkot (Feast of Tabernacles) סֻכּוֹת

1. Purpose: Sukkot commemorates the wanderings of the Children of Israel in the Wilderness after their deliverance from Egyptian bondage when they were compelled to dwell in huts or booths (Sukkah—booth; Lev. 23, 34). Occurring during the time of the fruit harvest it is also observed as a thanksgiving holyday, at the completion of the entire harvest, for the bounties of Nature during the previous year.

2. Date: The Festival has nine days (eight in Israel) and begins on the 15th of Tishri.

In addition to the first two days there are four intervening days (third to sixth inclusive) known as חוֹל הַמּוֹעֵד—weekdays of the Festival. There are three further days, with characteristics of their own making a combined nine day festival period.

3. Names:

(a) חַג הַסֻּכּוֹת Festival of Booths (Lev. 23, 34).

(b) חַג הָאָסִיף Festival of Ingathering (Exod. 23, 16).

(c) זְמַן שִׂמְחָתֵנוּ Season of our Rejoicing (Deut. 16, 14).

(d) חַג The Feast (Lev. 23, 39-41).

(e) The first two days are called Sukkot.

(f) The seventh day is called הוֹשַׁעְנָא רַבָּא—The Great Hoshana.

(g) The eighth day is called שְׁמִינִי עֲצֶרֶת—The Feast of the Eighth day or the Eighth Day of Solemn Assembly.

(h) The ninth day is called שִׂמְחַת תּוֹרָה—Rejoicing of the Law. (This day is really the second day of שְׁמִינִי עֲצֶרֶת).

4. Observances:

(a) **The Sukkah:** The Sukkah is a temporary structure especially built either in the yard, in the garden, or on the roof of the house. It is not covered from above with board but with detached branches so that the insubstantial nature of the physical structure may symbolise more clearly the dependence of man on God's protection. The historic significance of the Sukkah serves as a reminder of the booths or temporary dwellings in which Israel dwelt throughout its momentous journey in the Wilderness.

It is customary for pious Jews to drive in the first nail or stake for the erection of the Sukkah at the end of the Day of Atonement, and in this way the religious Jew indicates his love for Judaism which fills his whole life with the continuous performance of religious acts. The candles are lit in the Sukkah, the Kiddush is recited and meals during the Festival are eaten there.

(b) During the Festival the following four kinds of plants אַרְבָּעָה מִינִים are used in accordance with the Biblical command "to rejoice before the Lord,"—

    (i) a palm branch, לוּלָב

    (ii) three myrtle twigs, הֲדַסִּים

    (iii) two willow branches, עֲרָבוֹת

    (iv) and a citron, אֶתְרוֹג

Lulav is the word applied, for short, to all four elements which are arranged in a bouquet.

The Lulav is used on the first seven days, excepting the Sabbath. Because gladness is coupled with the festive branch, it is waved by the Chazan (Reader) in the synagogue service during the chanting of the Hallel prayers, in all directions, east, south, west, and north upwards and downwards, as an acknowledgment of God's sovereignty over the entire universe.

Processional circuits (הַקָּפוֹת), with the Chazan leading, are made around the reading desk or Bimah, while Hoshanot (הוֹשַׁעֲנוֹת) are chanted, as in the Temple. The word Hoshanah means "Save, we beseech Thee" and indicates the character of these public petitions to God. "Benshing" etrog, with the appropriate blessing at home or in the synagogue is performed during the first seven days of the Festival.

5. Hoshanah Rabba:

The Hoshanah is made up of small willow twigs tied together with strips of willow bark or palm leaf. It is used in the synagogue on the morning of Hoshanah Rabba (The Great Hoshanah), the seventh day of Sukkot. The procession around the Bimah is repeated seven times. At the last, with a petition for forgiveness of sins, each worshipper strikes his branch a few times on the desk or bench before him until a few leaves have fallen off, and then throws the twig away. This is intended as a symbol of the resurrection of life after death since the denuded branches of a tree take on new foliage in due season. Poetical prayers are recited, among them one full of Messianic hopes—

קוֹל מְבַשֵּׂר, מְבַשֵּׂר וְאוֹמֵר "A voice bringeth good tidings, and proclaimeth."

6. Shemini Atzeret and Simchat Torah—in the Synagogue

(*a*)   **Geshem:** The Musaph Service includes a prayer for גֶּשֶׁם (rain) on שְׁמִינִי עֲצֶרֶת—the Eighth Day of Solemn Assembly—this being the season when people in the Holy Land look forward to the coming rain, which is essential for a fruitful year. The prayer in the Diaspora may be regarded as a mark of unity with the land of Israel.

(*b*)   On the eve and on the morning of Simchat Torah הַקָּפוֹת (circuits) with the scrolls of the Law are made in the synagogue.

(*c*)   Children are encouraged to take part in these processions and carry flags with pictures of the Sefer Torah, Ten Commandments and Magen David on them. Fruits and sweets are distributed to the children.

(*d*)   Boys under Barmitzvah age are also called up to the Reading desk and after an adult has recited the blessing, a portion of the Law is read for them while a large Tallit is held over them like a canopy. This ceremony is called כָּל הַנְּעָרִים lit. "All the young boys."

(*e*)   Simchat Torah marks the completion of the one year cycle of the reading of the Law. But since Torah reading should be continuous, as soon as the final portion of the Law is read, a second Scroll is opened and a new cycle is commenced by reading the first part of Genesis.

(*f*)   A special ceremony attends the reading of the last and first sections of the Pentateuch. The persons who are honoured by being called up are designated חֲתַן תּוֹרָה (Bridegroom of the Law) and חֲתַן בְּרֵאשִׁית (Bridegroom of the Beginning).

IV

High Festivals

a. Rosh Hashanah (New Year) רֹאשׁ הַשָּׁנָה

1. **Introduction:** The Jewish New Year and Day of Atonement differ from other festivals in that they are more concerned with the individual and there is less national or historical significance associated with them than with other holy days in our Calendar. The New Year brings the individual before his God; its teaching touches upon ideas of sin, repentance and the ideal way of man on earth. Because these concepts are so fundamental the Festival is introduced by a period of preparation in which we can attune ourselves to the proper mood for the great day.

2. **The month of Elul and Selichot:** Throughout the month of Elul the Shofar is sounded on weekdays after the morning service to remind the worshipper of the forthcoming holy days. Further to inspire a mood of penitence, special "Selichot" or penitential prayers are recited as the Festival days draw near. The first "Selichot" service is held early Sunday morning in the week prior to the New Year, or better still at midnight when the stillness of the hour creates the atmosphere of solemnity suited to the penitential period.

3. **Date:** The Festival falls on the 1st and 2nd days of the Hebrew month of Tishri. From early times it was observed for two days, even in Palestine. In this, it is unlike those other festivals which are kept only for one day in Israel.

4. **Names:**

(a) רֹאשׁ הַשָּׁנָה   The New Year. This is the most popular name of all. Although it is the seventh month of the year, Tishri was regarded as most appropriate for spiritual reflection, since it is the autumn month in the land of its origin. Nature has finished the year's cycle; the harvests are gathered in and there is a short period of rest before the annual tasks are re-commenced. Further, it was taught by some that the act of the creation of the Universe was commenced at this time.

(b) יוֹם הַדִּין   The Day of Judgment. The Festival is an occasion for self-examination in the light of the teachings of our Religion. Our conscience is laid bare before God who is said to review each one of us in judgment.

(c) יוֹם הַזִּכָּרוֹן   The Day of Memorial. References are made in the Prayer Book to God who remembers every living creature on this "Day of Memorial."

(d) יוֹם תְּרוּעָה   The Day of Sounding the Shofar (Num. 29, 1). This is the original Biblical name for the Festival.

5. **Observances:** The observances of the day and the liturgy in the synagogue are designed to help us to reflect seriously upon the year gone by and to use the opportunity before we enter upon a new year to examine our failures and frailties in the light of the noble ideals laid down by our religion. Rosh Hashanah inaugurates a period of Ten Days of Penitence, which finds its climax on the 10th day—Yom Kippur.

6. **Customs in the Synagogue:**

(a) The Shofar is the most important symbol indicating the solemn lessons of this day and is sounded on both days of the Festival but not on a Sabbath. The purpose of sounding the Shofar has been well given by the great medieval Jewish teacher, Maimonides, who wrote that the notes of the Shofar are intended to proclaim the need for an immediate spiritual revival.

"Awake, ye sleepers, and ponder your deeds; remember your Creator and go back to Him in penitence. Be not of those who miss reality in their hunt after shadows; who waste their years in seeking after vain things which cannot profit or deliver. Look well to your souls and consider your acts; forsake each of you his evil ways and thoughts and return to God, that He may have mercy upon you."

There are several additional reasons for blowing the Shofar. Among these may be mentioned the following: The Shofar was sounded on all important occasions in the Jewish Calendar, such as the New Moon and the Jubilee Year. It reminds us of the giving of the Torah on Mount Sinai when the Shofar was sounded to mark the end of the Divine Revelation. It links the day with the sacrifice of Isaac, when a ram with curved horns appeared to take the place of Isaac on the altar. (The account of this sacrifice has had a central place in Jewish thought because it portrays the willingness of the Jew to "offer" himself to God's service.) Finally, the Shofar is a reminder of the Day of Judgment, of the coming of the Messiah and the Resurrection.

(b) The white vestments of the Scrolls of the Law and the Ark and the white robes worn by the ministers and occasionally by laymen also, represent the ideals of purity and nearness to God, and enhance the religious solemnities of the day.

7. Customs in the Home: A number of family customs for the home are associated with Rosh Hashanah and supply a delightful poetic touch to the observance of the Festival.

(a) **Apple and Honey:** After Kiddush on the Festival and before commencing the meal, a piece of apple is dipped in honey and eaten after saying an appropriate prayer for a good and sweet year. The prayer can be found on page 244 of the Singer's Prayer Book.

(b) Connected with the same custom we may note that sour or pickled foods are avoided on this day as being inappropriate to the nature of the Festival.

(c) It is customary for some seasonal fruit not eaten hitherto during the year to be kept aside for the second night of the Festival for the recital of שֶׁהֶחֱיָנוּ.

(d) In some households where the women bake their own bread it is usual to make the plaited crust shaped in the form of a ladder to signify our earnest aspirations upwards to God on those days.

8. General Customs:

(a) New Year Greeting cards have become very popular in recent times. The standard greeting for the Festival is לְשָׁנָה טוֹבָה תִּכָּתֵבוּ (Lit. "May you be inscribed for a good year").

(*b*)   An interesting custom that arose in the Middle Ages is the custom of Tashlich (תַּשְׁלִיךְ). In the afternoon of the first day (or on the second day if the first be a Sabbath) pious Jews go to the bank of a river and recite there some brief prayers and a passage from the Book of Micah containing a reference to the forgiving God who "casts our sins into the depths of the sea" (Tashlich—to cast). This is a figure of speech meaning that God is prepared to pardon our sins if we sincerely repent.

b. Yom Kippur *(Day of Atonement)*   יוֹם כִּפּוּר

1. **Purpose:** The principal object of the Day of Atonement is "Repentance"—this being brought about by a sincere desire to recognise our sins, to confess, to express regret, and to be prepared to abandon the path of wrongdoing. In accordance with the Biblical instruction, "Ye shall afflict your souls" (Lev. 23, 23-32) we abstain from all food and drink from sunset on the eve of the Day of Atonement until the beginning of the night of the following day.

2. **Date:** The Fast of the Day of Atonement commences on the eve of the 10th of Tishri at sunset and terminates at nightfall on the eve of the 11th.

3. **Services in the Synagogue:** There are five services during the day: Kol Nidrei, Morning, Additional, Afternoon and Neilah.

(*a*) **Kol Nidrei:**   The evening service of the Day of Atonement is preceded by the chanting of כָּל נִדְרֵי (Lit. "all vows") a prayer recited thrice, being a formal abrogation of all vows made during the past year. This affects only the obligations of man towards God but not those towards his fellow. The history of the text and the melody is clouded in mystery. Some scholars believe they derive from the period of the persecution in early medieval Spain.

(*b*) **Confession:**   The ritual of the day is replete with petitions for forgiveness for sins. A list of confessions is recited and prayers for pardon appear throughout the Prayer Book. According to Jewish teaching the Day of

Atonement brings forgiveness only for those sins committed against God. Transgressions committed against one's fellow must first be forgiven by the person who has been wronged.

(c) **Avodah;**

This forms part of the Musaph or additional service and is a record of the impressive rutual of Temple days when the High Priest alone entered the Holy of Holies on this most solemn day.

(d) **Neilah:**

The afternoon service is followed by נְעִילָה (Closure) a collection of prayers which are invested with special significance and impressiveness. The Ark remains open throughout this part of the Service and the Shofar is blown at its termination.

V

Minor Festivals

a. Chanukah חֲנוּכָּה

1. **Purpose:** When Palestine came under Syrian-Greek rule in 175 B.C.E. the Jews were persecuted and forbidden to practise their ancient faith. This led to a revolt instigated by an aged priest Mattathias, who, together with his sons and a poorly armed band of followers attempted to overthrow the enemy. After years of fighting, the Jews were temporarily successful and drove out the enemy. Mattathias had died in the meantime and his son Judah, better known as "The Maccabean" (from the initial letters of the motto מִי כָמֹכָה בָּאֵלִם יי on his banner) carried on the struggle. In celebration of the defeat of the enemy and the re-dedication of the desecrated Temple the Jews celebrate the Festival of Chanukah (Lit. "Dedication").

2. **Date:** Chanukah is celebrated for eight days from the 25th of Kislev.

3. **Names:**

   (a) חֲנוּכָּה means literally "dedication" and is the appropriate name of the Festival which commemorates the re-dedication of the Temple.

   An ingenious suggestion gives added significance to the term חנוכה which when divided into two parts makes חנו (they rested) כה (on the 25th).

   (b) חַג הָאוֹרִים The Festival of Lights, a name which describes the main feature of the Festival.

4. **Observance:** Commencing on the 25th of Kislev candles are kindled to proclaim the miracle of the Temple lights, when the cruse of oil containing only enough oil to last for one day sufficed for eight days, thus keeping alight the מְנוֹרָה or Candelabrum of the Temple

   (a) The lights are kindled as follows: On the first night the light on the right of the lamp is kindled. On the second night an extra light is added on the left and so on for eight nights. It is customary to have an extra light which acts as "shammash" or attendant light, with which to kindle the others. On Friday evening the Chanukah lights

22

are lit before the Sabbath candles and on the termination of the Sabbath, they are lit after Havdalah.

(*b*) **In the Synagogue:** Lights are kindled in the synagogue as well as in the home. Extra prayers are recited.

(*c*) **In the Home:** The lights should be lighted near a window or doorway in order that the commemoration of the miracle should be made public. מָעוֹז צוּר is a popular hymn sung after the kindling of the lights and from the initial letters of the verses is said to have been composed by a certain Mordecai. Parties are arranged for the children and gifts or "Chanukah gelt" (Chanukah money) distributed to them. Various games based on the story of Chanukah are played the most popular of which is played with a "dreidel," a small spinning "put and take" top on the sides of which are written the Hebrew letters נ׳ג׳ה׳ש indicating the phrase נֵס גָּדוֹל הָיָה שָׁם (A great miracle happened there).

b. *Purim*   פּוּרִים

1. **Purpose:** Purim is celebrated in commemoration of the deliverance of the Jews in Persia from the hands of Haman, the king's officer, who plotted their death.

2. **Date:** The 14th of Adar. The 15th of Adar is known as Shushan Purim since in the capital, Shushan, the Jews had to defend themselves against their enemies on the 14th and celebrated the Festival a day later.

3. **Name:** It is called Purim from the word פּוּר which means "lot" and refers to the evil machinations of Haman who cast lots to determine on which day he should arrange for the slaughter of the Jews of Persia.

4. **Observance:**

(*a*) **In the Synagogue:** On the eve of Purim and on Purim morning the Book of Esther, מְגִילַת אֶסְתֵּר is chanted to a special melody. At the mention of Haman the children stamp their feet or turn their "greggers" (sort of rattles) in derision of the name of the arch enemy.

(*b*) **In the Home:** Being a joyful Festival, Purim is the occasion for parties and celebrations. A festive meal, סְעוּדָה is the occasion for a happy family gathering. Charity is distributed and there is

מִשְׁלוֹחַ מָנוֹת an interchange of gifts, particularly food gifts, between friends and neighbours.

c. Lag B'Omer and Counting the Omer ל"ג בָּעֹמֶר

According to the Bible (Lev. 23, 11) an offering consisting of an "Omer" (a specific measure) of barley was brought to the Temple on the second day of Pesach. The Omer was, in fact, the yield of a sheaf of barley. From that day onwards it was necessary to count forty nine days until Shavuot—the Feast of the Wheat Harvest. After the destruction of the Temple the practice of bringing barley was discontinued but the Jews continued to "count the Omer period," a custom which has continued throughout the ages.

This period from Pesach to Shavuot has through the years become identified with sad memories for Jewry. Massacres occurred during the times of the Romans and later still during the Crusades. In the days of the Roman emperor Hadrian, the Jews—led by Bar Kochba—attempted to drive out the foreign oppressors from Judea. In this revolt they were unsuccessful and during the fighting thousands of Jews lost their lives. According to tradition numerous pupils of the saintly Rabbi Akiva died as a result of a plague that raged during the time of the "Sephirah" (Counting the Omer). For that reason it is customary nowadays to observe a period of semi-mourning during the days of the Counting of the Omer, generally during the whole month of Iyyar (May-June), when no weddings may be celebrated. On one day only, the thirty third day of the Omer corresponding to the 18th of Iyyar is this ban lifted, since the plague is said to have ceased on that day. This day is therefore known as "The Scholars Feast" and all festivities are permitted. It is known in Hebrew as ל"ג בָּעֹמֶר (Lag B'Omer—the thirty third day of the Omer); לג equals 33.

The Counting of the Omer takes place in the evening generally after the Evening Service.

d. New Year for Trees חֲמִשָּׁה עָשָׂר בִּשְׁבָט

1. **Purpose:** The minor Festival of Tu B'Shevat (15th Shevat) is one that is today celebrated mainly in Israel.

At this time of the year in Israel the winter has just passed and the sap is beginning to fill the trees with the promise of spring. It is the time of the year which was appropriately fixed for computing the annual tithes of fruit but its significance today is entirely as a nature festival which expresses the close ties binding Israel to the soil of the Holy Land.

2. **Date:** The New Year for Trees falls on the 15th day of Shevat.

3. **Names:**

(a) חֲמִשָּׁה עָשָׂר בִּשְׁבָט 15th of Shevat.

(b) ט״ו בִּשְׁבָט ט״ו has the numerical value of 15.

(c) רֹאשׁ הַשָּׁנָה לָאִילָנוֹת New Year for Trees.

4. **Observance:** The Festival has no special observances though the custom still prevails of eating fruits that grow in Eretz Yisrael. Within recent years however, the day has risen to more prominence even in the Diaspora as a result of the large scale educational activities of the Jewish National Fund which has brought the message of the land to Jews the world over.

e. Rosh Chodesh רֹאשׁ חֹדֶשׁ

1. **Observance in former times:**

At one time the day of the New Moon was fixed by actual observation of the moon. As soon as it was visible the Sanhedrin (Supreme Rabbinical Court) in Palestine was informed and after ascertaining that the information was correct the day of the New Moon (Rosh Chodesh) was announced. This system of direct observation was later discarded in favour of a more permanent method.

2. **The Fixed Calendar:**

It was Hillel II (c. 360 C.E.) who framed the fixed calendar which is in use to the present day.

3. **The Sabbath of Blessing:** (שַׁבָּת מְבָרְכִין)

The practice at the present time is to herald the arrival of the New Moon by reciting a number of prayers on the Sabbath previous to the new month. The date or dates on which the new month commences are announced. This Sabbath is known as (שַׁבָּת מְבָרְכִין) (S.P.B. p. 154).

4. Sanctification of the Moon: קִדּוּשׁ לְבָנָה

It is customary to consecrate or sanctify the new moon some time during the first part of the month when the moon is visible. This generally takes place at the termination of the Sabbath. The order of service regulating this old ceremony is not found in the Singer's Prayer Book but may be looked up in a more comprehensive edition of the Prayer Book.

f. Yom Ha'atzmaut (Israel Independence Day) יוֹם הָעַצְמָאוּת

On Iyyar 5th, 1948, the elected and representative Jewish leaders in Palestine solemnly proclaimed the establishment of the State of Israel. The birth of the third independent Jewish State in history was brought about after several decades of intensive Zionist efforts culminating in the historic 1947 declaration of the United Nations in favour of a Jewish State in Palestine. Thus the 2000 years of Jewish prayer, hope and waiting for a national return to an independent homeland have at last been realised.

The anniversary of the declaration of Israel independence is celebrated as Yom Ha'atzmaut יום העצמאות (Independence Day), and recently the rabbinic authorities have allowed a relaxation of the laws of semi-mourning which are traditionally observed during that part of the "Sephira" so that Independence Day can be celebrated as a joyous holiday.

The main centre of festivities is naturally in the Land of Israel. But Jewish communities all over the world feel closely bound to the problems and achievements of the young State, so that Independence Day is now a notable day in the calendar of Jewish people all over the world.

The regular features of organised celebrations for the day include special services of thanksgiving and youth displays which portray aspects of Israeli life.

In Israel itself, Yom Ha'atzmaut is observed as a public holiday. The day before is kept as a יוֹם זִכָּרוֹן, a day of commemoration for those who died in the successful defence of their new-born State when the surrounding Arab States attacked Israel.

GENERAL

VI

The Special Sabbaths

1. **The Four Special Sabbaths**: From the period between the end of the Hebrew month of Shevat and the beginning of the month of Nisan there are four Special Sabbaths, each one of which is distinguished by a special additional passage read from the Torah.

(a) שַׁבַּת שְׁקָלִים   **The Sabbath of the Shekels.** The portion of the Law dealing with the half-shekel contribution is read (Exod. 30, 11-16). This portion is read on the Sabbath before the 1st of Adar, or on the 1st should it be a Sabbath. The custom is associated with the half shekel tax which was due at this time of the year.

(b) שַׁבַּת זָכוֹר   **The Sabbath of Remembrance.** This occurs on the Sabbath before Purim when the portion referring to the enmity of Amalek for Israel is read (Deut. 25, 17-19). Since Haman was descended from Amalek the portion is appropriate for the period approaching Purim.

(c) שַׁבַּת פָּרָה   **The Sabbath of the Red Heifer.** On the Sabbath after Purim the portion dealing with the sacrifice of the red heifer is read, a reminder of the importance of purity. This reading receives prominence at the approach of Passover since in Temple days a state of ritual impurity would debar a person from taking part in the Festival sacrifice (Numb. 19).

(d) שַׁבַּת הַחֹדֶשׁ **The Sabbath of the Month.** This is the Sabbath before the 1st of Nisan or on the 1st of Nisan if that day be a Sabbath. The portion dealing with the command that Nisan be the first month is read (Exod. 12, 1-20).

Besides these four Special Sabbaths there are a number of other Sabbaths which are distinguished by a special name:

(i) שַׁבָּת הַגָּדוֹל **The Great Sabbath.** The Sabbath immediately prior to the **Festival of Pesach,** so called for a number of reasons:

(a) It is probable that the Sabbath before every festival was called the Great Sabbath though in time the name was restricted to the Sabbath before the Passover, on which important instructions were given concerning the Festival.

(b) Tradition has it that the 10th of Nisan in the year of the Exodus when the Israelites were commanded to set aside the Paschal lamb was a Sabbath.

(c) There is an association with the Haftarah of the day which refers to the "Great Day of the Lord" (Malachi 3).

(ii) שַׁבָּת חָזוֹן **The Sabbath of the Vision.** The Sabbath preceding the Fast of Av is called CHAZON since the Haftarah read is the first chapter of the book of Isaiah commencing with the word CHAZON.

(iii) שַׁבָּת נַחֲמוּ **The Sabbath of Comfort.** The Sabbath following the 9th of Av when the

VI.—*The Special Sabbaths*

portion read for the Haftarah is taken from Isaiah 40 commencing with the word NACHAMU.

(iv) שַׁבָּת שׁוּבָה — **The Sabbath of Repentance.** The Sabbath between the New Year and the Day of Atonement (Rosh Hashanah and Yom Kippur) is so called because the Haftarah read commences with the word SHUVA (repent) Hosea, 14. 2.

(v) שַׁבָּת בְּרֵאשִׁית — The Sabbath following the Feast of Tabernacles is so called since on that Sabbath the first portion of the Pentatateuch is read and the annual cycle of readings is re-commenced.

VII

The Minor Fasts

There are a number of Minor Fasts in the Jewish Calendar. They are listed here in the order in which they occur in the calendar.

Nisan: 14th: תַּעֲנִית בְּכוֹרִים

Fast of the Firstborn. A symbolic fast of thanksgiving in commemoration of the deliverance of the Israelites' firstborn when the Egyptian firstborn were slain prior to the departure of the Jews from Egypt.

Tammuz: 17th:

שִׁבְעָה־עָשָׂר בְּתַמּוּז

The fast of the 17th of Tammuz. This commemorates a number of events:

(*a*) The breaching of the walls of Jerusalem by the Romans (c. 70 C.E.).

(*b*) Tradition has it that Moses broke the two tablets of the Law on the 17th of Tammuz.

(*c*) A Greek, Apostomos, burnt the Torah.

(*d*) The regular daily sacrifice ceased in the Temple.

The 17th of Tammuz ushers in the Three Weeks of National mourning till the 9th of Av, during which the pious abstain from every kind of enjoyment.

Av: 9th: תִּשְׁעָה בְּאָב

The Fast of the 9th of Av. This is more of a major than a minor fast since it commemorates:

(*a*) The Destruction of both the First and the Second Temples (586 B.C.E. and 70 C.E.).

(*b*) The fall of Bethar in the Bar-Kochba rebellion (135 C.E.).

(*c*) In later centuries other sad occurrences were associated with this day: perhaps the most tragic is the Expulsion of the Jews from Spain in 1492.

The severity of the 9th of Av equals that of the Day of Atonement in that both fast days commence on the previous evening. The synagogue presents a gloomy appearance, for the lights are dimmed, the curtain is removed from the Ark and the worshippers sit on low stools or on the floor. קִינוֹת (Prayers of lamentation) are recited and אֵיכָה—The Book of Lamentations is read. The Tallit and Tephillin are not worn during the morning service, instead they are worn in the afternoon service. Only essential work is permitted.

The Kinot: These prayers tell of the glory that was Israel's and the martyrdom undergone by our ancestors who gave their lives for their Faith. There are some 40 Kinot many of which were composed by Yehuda Halevi (1085-1140) the renowned Spanish-Jewish poet.

Tishri: 3rd: צוֹם גְּדַלְיָה   The Fast of Gedaliah. A fast commemorating the murder of Gedaliah, a scion of the royal house of Judah who had been appointed governor of Judea by Nebuchadnezzar and whose assassination led to further trouble for the Jews living under Babylonian rule.

Tevet: 10th: עֲשָׂרָה בְּטֵבֵת   The Fast of the 10th of Tevet, the date on which Nebuchadnezzar commenced his siege of Jerusalem.

31

Adar: 13th: תַּעֲנִית אֶסְתֵּר   The Fast of Esther. A fast day instituted in memory of Queen Esther's fast before she pleaded with the king for her people.

Note:

4 days are kept as Fast days during the year to commemorate events connected with the fall of Jerusalem. In the Bible they are called (Zech. 8, 19)

"The Fast of the 4th month" ......17th Tammuz

"The Fast of the 5th month" ......9th of Av

"The Fast of the 7th month" ......3rd of Tishri

"The Fast of the 10th month" ......10th of Tevet

VIII

Kashrut and the Dietary Laws

A. Sources: Leviticus 11 and Deuteronomy 14 contain the basic laws regulating Jewish diet. Additional points were later developed by the rabbis.

B. The Main Regulations: These may be clearly seen under three main headings:

(a) The distinction between permitted and prohibited animals, fish and fowl.

(b) The prohibition against eating blood.

(c) The prohibition against the mixing of meat and milk.

C. Details:

(a) The Bible declares those animals clean which are cloven hoofed and chew the cud. Animals which have neither sign or only one sign are prohibited for food (e.g. swine).

Only fish which have scales and fins are permitted. In the case of fowl no distinguishing signs are given in the Bible. Instead, an illustrative list of unclean birds is given. From this, the rabbis have been able to deduce that birds of prey are prohibited as well as those which live and associate with known unclean birds.

(b) The prohibition against eating blood is one of the fundamental rules in the dietary code. The blood represents the life of the animal and it is regarded as a loathsome and irreligious act to eat the life blood under any circumstances. Under this head we might touch upon **Shechitah** as a method of Jewish slaughter of animals and fowl. By this method, which is carried out by a highly skilled שׁוֹחֵט who uses a knife of extreme sharpness, the vital veins of the throat are speedily severed, the animal is rendered unconscious and there is an abundant loss of blood through the cut. Shechitah thus does two things. It is extremely humane as a method of slaughter since the cut is done so quickly that the animal becomes unconscious within seconds, suffering no pain. Secondly, by the profuse bleeding most of the blood is drained from the animal and so the prohibition against the eating the blood of the animal can be effectively observed. An additional safe-guard is the porging of meat (removal of forbidden fat and blood veins). This is carried out by an expert before the meat is sold.

But this is not sufficient, since the housewife, on bringing the meat home must still **Kasher** the meat, i.e. render it perfectly pure from blood. This is done by soaking it in water for half an hour, then covering it all over with salt and allowing it to remain for an hour and then rinsing the meat with fresh water. Liver is made Kosher first by cutting it across several times then sprinkling it with salt and roasting it in an open fire.

(c) The Bible expressly forbids the cooking of meat and milk foods together. This regulation has been safeguarded in a way that enjoins the Jew to keep all meat and milk foods and utensils separate.

After a meat meal no milk products are eaten within a period of hours. After milk foods meat may be eaten shortly after since milk foods are easily digested.

D. Miscellaneous Food Laws:

(a) "All winged swarming things that go upon all fours are a detestable thing to you" (Lev. 11, 20).

"Every creeping thing that creeps upon the earth shall be an abomination" (Lev. 11,41). This includes crabs, oysters and lobsters.

(b) Eggs and milk of "unclean" animals or birds are forbidden. Roe of unclean fish is forbidden (i.e. caviare from the sturgeon).

(c) Gelatine made from the bones and hoofs of animals is forbidden.

(d) Certain fats are forbidden: generally the fat covering the inwards (Lev. 3, 3-4). This is known as חֵלֶב. Permitted fat is known as שׁוּמָן.

(e) A blood speck in an egg renders it unfit for food.

(f) The sinew of the hip (גִּיד הַנָּשֶׁה) a prohibition based on the command in the Torah reminding us of Jacob's wrestling with the angel (Gen. 32, 33). The "sinew that shrank" must be removed from the animal before it is used for food.

E. Reasons for their Observance: Many and various reasons for the Jewish dietary laws have been given. Here we shall mention only three.

VIII.—*Kashrut and the Dietary Laws*

(*a*)   **Religious:** The Bible proclaims "Ye shall be holy, for I am holy," and the association of the clean and pure with the ideal of holiness places Kashrut from this point of view in an area of teaching which is specifically religious.

(*b*)   **Self Restraint and Discipline:** Observance of these laws creates a character trained in its bodily appetites to discriminate between that which is permitted and that which for one reason or another Jewish teaching regards as unclean.

(*c*)   **Health:** It has been shown that observance of Kashrut is conducive to health. Certainly, the Shochet is an expert in his work and after Shechitah he carefully examines all the vital organs to see that the animal is absolutely free from any disease.

IX

A Classified Terminology
of the more important Hebrew Terms in everyday use

CONTENTS

Synagogue
Home
Prayer
Dietary Laws
Calendar
Festivals
Festivals (General terms)
Sabbaths
Special Sabbaths
Fasts
From the Cradle to the Grave
Education and Hebrew Literature
Ethics

Note: Many of the Hebrew Terms in the following pages are treated more fully in their appropriate section of the book and should be consulted there.

The Synagogue

Bet Haknesset:
בֵּית הַכְּנֶסֶת
The House of Assembly. A term applied to the synagogue proper. It is also called בֵּית תְּפִלָּה House of Prayer.

Bet Hamidrash:
בֵּית הַמִּדְרָשׁ
House of Study. The term applied to a room usually attached to a Synagogue for the purpose of study. (These days the room is also often used for prayer during the week.)

Bimah: בִּימָה — The platform in a synagogue on which the Law is read and from which the Reader leads the congregation in prayer.

Aron Hakodesh: אֲרוֹן הַקֹּדֶשׁ — The Holy Ark. The Ark in western countries occupies the centre of the east side of the synagogue and houses the scrolls of the Torah.

Petichah: פְּתִיחָה — Opening. Generally the opening of the Ark. This term is also applied to the opening of the Selichot (cf. **High Festivals**).

Ner Tamid: נֵר תָּמִיד — Continual or Everlasting Light. The light that burns in the synagogue continually in front of the Ark. It is symbolic of the light of the Torah before which it hangs and also a reminder of the Temple Candelabrum.

Sefer Torah: סֵפֶר תּוֹרָה — The Book of the Law. The handwritten scroll of the Torah from which readings are made.

Kriat Hatorah: קְרִיאַת הַתּוֹרָה — Reading of the Law. The Law is read four times weekly; Monday and Thursday mornings, Saturday morning and afternoon. On holydays, including Chanukah, Purim, Rosh Chodesh and fast days it is also read.

Yad: יָד — Hand. The pointer used by the Reader when reading from the scroll of the Law.

Aliyah: עֲלִיָּה — Going up. A term used when one is called up to the reading of the Law.

Sidrah: סִדְרָא — The portion of the Law read every Sabbath morning in the synagogue.

Maftir: מַפְטִיר — Concluding. The last portion of the sidrah is known as Maftir.

Haftarah: הַפְטָרָה — Conclusion. The portion selected from the books of the Prophets and read after the reading of the Law on Sabbaths, holydays and on fast days in the afternoon service.

Hagbahah: הַגְבָּהָה — Lifting. The ritual of lifting up the scroll after the reading of the Law.

Gelilah: גְּלִילָה — Rolling and binding up. The ceremony of binding up the scroll after the reading of the Law.

General

Chumash: חוּמָשׁ   Literally, "a fifth." The term used when referring to the Five Books of Moses or Pentateuch.

Siddur: סִדּוּר   Order. The Prayer Book is called an Order of Prayers.

Tallit: טַלִּית   Shawl. The prayer shawl or robe used by males during prayers.

Tzibur: צִבּוּר   Congregation or community. A term generally used is "Tefillah B'tzibur" (Prayer with a Minyan). Public prayer is regarded of greater worth than private prayer. Another term for congregation is קָהָל.

Minyan: מִנְיָן   Quorum or number. 10 males over the age of 13 constitute a congregation when public worship may be introduced. The minimum number forming a "congregation" is ten.

Home

Chanukat Habayit:
חֲנוּכַּת הַבַּיִת   Dedication or consecration of the house. A ceremony generally performed when one dedicates a new home (S.P.B. p. 300).

Mezuzah: מְזוּזָה   Door-post symbol. An outward sign of God's presence and a sanctification of the dwelling place. The Mezuzah is a piece of parchment on which are written the first two paragraphs of the Shema. This is rolled into a case and fixed on to the right hand doorpost in the top third section.

Hadlakot Nerot:
הַדְלָקַת נֵרוֹת   Kindling of the Lights. The ceremony performed by the mistress of the household on the eve of Sabbaths and holydays.

Kiddush: קִדּוּשׁ   Sanctification. Prayer over the wine recited on Sabbaths and holydays. In the absence of wine, Kiddush may be recited over bread.

Havdalah:
הַבְדָּלָה   Separation. The ceremony with wine, or other liquids (except water), spices and a light which bids farewell to the Sabbath and thus makes a separation or division between the sacred

day and the week. A shortened form of Havdalah is also recited on the termination of festivals.

Prayer

Siddur: סִדּוּר   Order. The Prayer Book.

Machzor: מַחְזוֹר   Cycle. The Festival Prayer Book.

Shachrit: שַׁחֲרִית   The Morning Prayer.

Minchah: מִנְחָה   The Afternoon Prayer.

Maariv or Arvit: The Evening Prayer.
מַעֲרִיב עַרְבִית

Musaph: מוּסָף   The additional prayers on Sabbath and holydays.

Hallel: הַלֵּל   Praise. Hymns of praise consisting of a number of Psalms and recited on certain festive days in the year (S.P.B. p. 219).

Pesuke D'zimra: Verses of song. The chief group of Psalms read at the beginning of the morning service (S.P.B. pp. 16-33).
פְּסוּקֵי דְזִמְרָא

Shema: שְׁמַע   The Shema is one of the central sections of the Prayer Book. It comprises three paragraphs: Deut. 6, 4-9: 11, 13-21: and Numb. 15, 37-41. It is recited twice daily (S.P.B. p. 40).

Amidah: עֲמִידָה   The name by which the prayer of the Eighteen Blessings or שמונה עשרה is known. The term עמידה (Prayer said standing) actually applies to the ordinary weekday Amidah which originally contained 18 Benedictions and now contains 19. "Amidah" is however used with reference to every such service on weekdays, Sabbaths and festivals.

Kedushah: קְדוּשָׁה   Holiness. In all formal services in the synagogue except the evening service, the Amidah is recited aloud in whole or in part by the Reader. At the end of the third paragraph

the Reader and congregation recite the
קדושה which is a poetic proclamation of
the sanctity of God (S.P.B. p. 45).

Mizrach: מִזְרָח   East. When praying in western countries the
Jew faces the east i.e. facing Jerusalem.

Arba Kanfot: The Four Corners. (Deut. 22, 12). The term
אַרְבַּע כַּנְפוֹת   usually applied to the four-cornered ritual
undergarment worn by male Jews.

Tzizit: צִיצִית   Fringe or Tassel. The four-cornered garment
provided with fringes worn by males. One of
the most important of the outward signs of
God's presence.

Tallit: טַלִּית   See Section on Synagogue.

Tephillin: Ornaments or Phylacteries. The wearing of
תְּפִילִין   Tephillin is incumbent upon every Jewish
male from the age of 13. The Tephillin con-
sist of two cases (Batim-houses), of which one
is placed on the head and is divided into four
compartments and the other, strapped on the
arm, has one compartment. Each case has a
Retzuah (strap) attached to it. Four paragraphs from the Torah, in each of which
mention is made of the Tephillin "signs", are
written on the parchment. In the head
Tephillin they are written on four separate
pieces of parchment, while in the arm Tephillin
they are all on one piece. The four paragraphs
are as follows:

(i) Deuteronomy 6, 4-9: Shema, the Unity
of God.

(ii) Deuteronomy 11, 13-20: The doctrine of
Divine righteousness.

(iii) Exodus 13, 1-10: Sanctification of the
Firstborn.

(iv) Exodus 13, 11-16: Reminder of the
deliverance from Egypt.

Tephillin are worn during the weekday morning services. At one time the pious wore Tephillin the whole day.

Alenu: עָלֵינוּ The Alenu prayer which is read at the end of all services is one of the most important prayers in the Prayer Book. It contains a declaration of Israel's uniqueness as a religious community set apart from other people and proceeds with a proclamation of God as supreme King of the Universe (S.P.B. p. 76).

Yigdal: יִגְדַּל The Thirteen Principles of the Jewish Faith appear in two forms in the Prayer Book. The prose form known as שְׁלֹשָׁה עָשָׂר עִקָּרִים (cf. S.P.B. pp. 2, 89) was set down by Maimonides. Later an unknown poet adopted this into the poetical form of Yigdal.

Adon Olam: אֲדוֹן עוֹלָם Lord of the World. One of the most popular hymns in the liturgy (S.P.B. p. 3). It contains the Jewish belief in a God who created all things from the beginning and who exercises his care over each individual.

Birkat Hamazon: בִּרְכַּת הַמָּזוֹן The Blessing for Food. The Grace after Meals (S.P.B. p. 278).

Dietary Laws

Kasher: כָּשֵׁר All food permitted in Jewish law is described as being Kasher, or fit for use.

Trefah: טְרֵיפָה Torn. Any food forbidden in Jewish law is described as being Trefah. The literal meaning is "torn."

Shechitah: שְׁחִיטָה Slaughter. The term applied to the Jewish method of slaughtering animals and fowl for food.

Neveilah: נְבֵלָה Carrion or carcase. An animal that has died a natural death or was not slaughtered according to ritual law. Such an animal is forbidden.

41

General

Basar B'chalav:

בָּשָׂר בְּחָלָב

Meat and milk. Jewish law forbids the cooking of milk and meat foods together or eating such foods together and it is usual to wait a number of hours after partaking of meat before eating milk foods.

Calendar

See Section 1.

Festivals

Passover

Bedikat Chametz:

בְּדִיקַת חָמֵץ

Searching for leavened bread. The ceremony generally performed by the head of the household on the eve of the 14th of Nisan.

Bi'ur Chametz:

בְּעוּר חָמֵץ

Burning of the Chametz. Destruction or removal of the Chametz. All leaven bread left after the first meal on the 14th day of Nisan must be destroyed.

Matza: מַצָּה

Unleavened bread.

Matza Shemurah:

מַצָּה שְׁמוּרָה

Matzot which are specially prepared or "guarded" for Passover from the earliest stage of the wheat grinding.

Maror: מָרוֹר

Bitter herbs.

Charoset: חֲרוֹסֶת

The mixture of nuts, fruit, wine and other ingredients used as an important symbol in the Seder ritual.

Seder: סֵדֶר

Order. The service for the first two nights of Passover.

Haggadah: הַגָּדָה

The name given to the book which contains the order of service for the two Seder nights.

Arba Kosot:

אַרְבַּע כּוֹסוֹת

The four cups. The four cups of wine used during the Seder.

Kos Shel Eliyahu:

כּוֹס שֶׁל אֵלִיָּהוּ

Elijah's cup (cf. Section 3A).

42

IX.—A Classified Terminology

Afikoman: אֲפִיקוֹמָן — Dessert (cf. Section 3A).

Tal: טַל — Dew. Prayer for dew recited on the first day of Passover during the additional service.

Feast of Weeks

Sheloshet Yemei Hagbalah: שְׁלֹשֶׁת יְמֵי הַגְבָּלָה — The three days of making bounds or borders. The three days preceding the giving of the Law when the Israelites were forbidden to come near Mount Sinai. The term still applies to the three days prior to Shavuot.

Tabernacles

Sukkah: סֻכָּה — Booth.

Lulav: לוּלָב — Palm. Branch of palm tree used during the Festival.

Aravot: עֲרָבוֹת — Willow branches attached to the Lulav.

Hadassim: הֲדַסִּים — Myrtle branches. Used during the Festival and attached to the Lulav.

Etrog: אֶתְרוֹג — Citron. One of the four kinds of plants used during the Festival.

Hoshana Rabba: הוֹשַׁעְנָא רַבָּא — The Great Hoshana. The name given to the seventh day of the Festival.

Shemini Atzeret: שְׁמִינִי עֲצֶרֶת — Eighth day of Solemn Assembly. The eighth day of Tabernacles.

Simchat Torah: שִׂמְחַת תּוֹרָה — Rejoicing of the Law. The ninth day of Tabernacles. The last day of the Festival when the reading of the Pentateuch is completed and re-commenced.

Chatan Torah: חֲתַן תּוֹרָה — Bridegroom of the Law. Honour bestowed on a member of the congregation on Simchat Torah who is called to the reading of the last portion of the Torah.

43

Chatan Bereshit: חֲתַן בְּרֵאשִׁית

Bridegroom of the first portion of the Torah. Honour bestowed on the person who is called to the reading of the first paragraph of Genesis on Simchat Torah.

Siyum: סִיּוּם

Conclusion. The custom of completing a Talmudic tractate with a discourse, followed by refreshments (or banquet).

High Festivals

Selichot: סְלִיחוֹת

Prayers of forgiveness. The additional prayers recited during the services of the week preceding the New Year.

Yamim Noraim: יָמִים נוֹרָאִים

Solemn Days. Name given to the days of Rosh Hashanah and Yom Kippur.

Aseret Yemei Teshuvah: עֲשֶׂרֶת יְמֵי תְּשׁוּבָה

The 10 days of Penitence. Another name given to the ten days from Tishri 1st to the 10th.

Shofar: שׁוֹפָר

Horn, trumpet. The ram's horn blown on the New Year and at the termination of the Day of Atonement. It is also sounded daily during the month of Elul.

Tekiah, Shevarim, Teruah: תְּקִיעָה, שְׁבָרִים, תְּרוּעָה

The three different types of Shofar sounds.

Leshanah Tovah Tikkatevu: לְשָׁנָה טוֹבָה תִּכָּתֵבוּ

"May you be inscribed for a good year." The greeting made by Jews to one another at the New Year.

Kol Nidrei: כָּל נִדְרֵי

All vows. The opening paragraph recited thrice on the eve of the Day of Atonement.

Vidui: וִדּוּי

Confession. The confession of sins which is a central feature in the services of Yom Kippur.

Maftir Yonah:
מַפְטִיר יוֹנָה

The prophetical book of Jonah which is read during the afternoon service on Yom Kippur.

Neilah: נְעִילָה

Closure. The final prayers said on the Day of Atonement.

Festivals (General)

Yom Tov:
יוֹם טוֹב

"A good day." Name given to a festival or holyday.

Chol Hamoed:
חוֹל הַמּוֹעֵד

The weekday or ordinary day of a festival. The intermediate days of the Festivals of Passover and Tabernacles.

Isru Chag:
אִסְרוּ חַג

"Bind the festival." The day following a festival is so called. It is kept as a semi-festive occasion in the sense that certain prayers usually recited on ordinary weekdays are omitted.

Chamesh Megillot:
חָמֵשׁ מְגִילוֹת

The five scrolls. Five books of the Bible which are read on special occasions.

(i) Song of Songs ......Passover.

(ii) Ruth ....Feast of Weeks.

(iii) Lamentations ....Fast of Av.

(iv) Ecclesiastes ....Tabernacles.

(v) Esther ....Purim.

Eruv Tavshillin:
עֵירוּב תַּבְשִׁילִין

Combination of dishes. Should a Sabbath follow a holyday it is permitted to prepare food for the Sabbath on the holyday provided such preparation has commenced on the eve of the holyday. Thus the preparation is said to continue on the Yom Tov and has not just commenced. The food prepared (the Eruv Tavshillin) is usually eaten at the third Sabbath meal (Shalosh Seudot).

General

Sabbaths

Kabbalat Shabbat:
קַבָּלַת שַׁבָּת

Receiving the Sabbath. The Friday evening Psalms recited before the actual evening service are so called. Generally this term refers to the whole Service since it ushers in the Sabbath.

Lecha Dodi:
לְכָה דוֹדִי

"Come my beloved." One of the important hymns sung during the Friday eve service. Written in the form of an acrostic and composed by Solomon Halevi Alkabetz (16th century).

Kiddush: קִדּוּשׁ

Sanctification. The prayer over wine recited in the synagogue and at home on Friday evening.

Zemirot: זְמִירוֹת

Sabbath hymns sung at intervals during the meals on Sabbath.

Shalosh Seudot:
שָׁלשׁ סְעוּדוֹת

The Three Meals. The three main meals eaten on the Sabbath:
(i) Friday evening.
(ii) Sabbath lunch.
(iii) Sabbath afternoon. Generally the third meal is known by this name.

Havdalah:
הַבְדָּלָה

Separation. The benediction over a cup of wine (on Saturday night also with spices and lighted taper) recited at the termination of the Sabbath and festivals.

Special Sabbaths

See Section 6 for an explanation of the various special Sabbaths.

IX.—A Classified Terminology

From the Cradle to the Grave

B'rit Milah:
בְּרִית מִילָה

Covenant of Circumcision. The ceremony of circumcision by which every male child is initiated into the Covenant of Abraham (Lev. 12, 3) on the eighth day of birth. If for medical reasons it cannot be carried out on the eighth day then the circumcision may be postponed.

Pidyon Habben:
פִּדְיוֹן הַבֵּן

Redemption of the son (the firstborn). A ceremony at which a male firstborn is redeemed on the thirty first day of his birth. This ceremony does not apply to children of Kohanim or Levites or to children of mothers who are the daughters of Kohanim or Levites (S.P.B. p. 308).

Bar-Mitzvah:
בַּר מִצְוָה

Son of a Commandment. Following his 13th birthday a boy is called up in the synagogue to read a portion of the Law. At the age of 13 he reaches his religious majority and Jewish law recognises his responsibility under the Law from then onwards.

Erusin and Kiddushin:
אֵירוּסִין
קִידוּשִׁין

Betrothal and Marriage. The constituent parts of the marriage ceremony.

Chatan and Kallah:
חָתָן־כַּלָּה

Bridegroom and Bride.

Chuppah: חוּפָּה

Canopy. This term is also generally applied to the actual ceremony. The Bride and Bridegroom stand together under a canopy during the ceremony. It may indicate their ideal union. Modern writers often refer to it as the symbol of God's presence over the bridal couple or as the symbol of the Sanctuary whose ideal purity and holiness should characterise the home about to be set up.

47

Ketubah: כְּתוּבָה
Marriage Contract. A document (in Aramaic) read at the marriage service, an abstract of which is generally printed on the other side in English, and which contains a statement of the obligations of husband and wife towards each other.

Sheva Berachot: שֶׁבַע בְּרָכוֹת
Seven Blessings. The seven benedictions of wedlock which are chanted by the Reader at the end of the marriage service.

Get: גֵּט
Divorce. The document of divorce, necessary to comply with Jewish law.

Chevra Kadisha: חֶבְרָא קַדִּישָׁא
Holy Brotherhood. Usually the organisation which carries out the holy rites appertaining to burial according to Jewish law and tradition.

Taharah: טָהֳרָה
Purification. The ceremony of washing and robing the dead body in accordance with the last rites.

Avel: אָבֵל
Mourner. Term applied to mourners during the full year of mourning.
Before the burial the mourner is known as an **Onan.**

Keriah: קְרִיעָה
Rending. The custom of rending the garment —performed by near relatives before the burial as a sign of deep grief.

Shiva: שִׁבְעָה
Seven. The seven days of mourning after the burial during which the mourners remain in their homes.

Sheloshim: שְׁלשִׁים
Thirty. The thirty days of full mourning after which the bereaved observe a period of semi-mourning till the expiration of eleven months.

Yahrzeit: יאָהרצייט
Anniversary of a death. The word is not Hebrew but Yiddish (from the German).

Kaddish: קַדִּישׁ
Sanctification. The prayer recited by mourners during the period of mourning and on the anniversary of a death.

Matzevah: מַצֵּבָה   Memorial or Tombstone. A tombstone is usually set up over the grave of a relative some 12 months after the death and is unveiled at a special ceremony. A Matzevah is first mentioned with reference to the death of Rachel when Jacob placed a memorial on her grave.

Education and Hebrew Literature

Tanach: תנ"ך   Bible. A word made up of the three initial letters T (Torah): N (Neviim-Prophets): CH (Ketuvim-Writings). These three sections constitute the whole of the Bible.

Masorah: מָסוֹרָה   Tradition. From the time of Ezra the text of the Bible was subject to most careful and painstaking examination with a view to the elimination of errors that careless copying had brought into numerous copies of the Bible. The scholars responsible were called Masorites and they aimed at the creation of a uniform and correct text. Their corrections and observations were embodied in a series of marginal or separate notes.

Halachah L'Moshe Misinai: הֲלָכָה לְמֹשֶׁה מִסִּינַי   Literally, a law transmitted to Moses from Sinai. Any extremely ancient law or custom whose origin, while not fully understood, is believed to go back to days of antiquity.

Aseret Hadibrot: עֲשֶׂרֶת הַדִּבְּרוֹת   The Ten words or Ten Commandments.

Taryag: תַּרְיַ"ג   A group of letters whose numerical value is 613. An abbreviation for the 613 Commandments in the Torah; 248 Positive and 365 Negative commandments.

Mishnah: מִשְׁנָה

Learning. The Oral Law was written down about 200 C.E. and put into its present order by Rabbi Judah Hanasi.

Gemara: גְּמָרָא

Completion. The discussion on the Mishnah (cf. Talmud).

Talmud: תַּלְמוּד

The Gemara is in the nature of a discussion on the Mishnah. Together they are called **Talmud** (lesson). The Talmud contains laws, narratives, history, fables, allegories, meditations, prayers, ethics, moral sayings, philosophical and religious discussions. There are 63 books of the Talmud collected in 6 main sections (שׁשׁה סדרים—or six orders) as follows:

1. זְרָעִים Agricultural laws and Divine worship.

2. מוֹעֵד Sabbath and Festivals.

3. נָשִׁים Laws appertaining to women.

4. נְזִיקִין Civil and criminal law.

5. קָדָשִׁים Laws dealing with sacrifices.

6. טָהֲרוֹת Cleanliness and purifications.

There are two Talmuds; the Jerusalem and the Babylonian. The one in popular use is the Babylonian, תַּלְמוּד בַּבְלִי. The Jerusalem or Palestinian Talmud is much smaller and is not as authoritative as the Babylonian version. A mnemonic for the 6 sections is

זְמַ'ן נָ'קַ'ט Zeman Nakat.

Anshe Knesset Hagdolah: אַנְשֵׁי כְּנֶסֶת הַגְּדוֹלָה

The Men of the Great Synagogue or Synod. An assembly of some 120 scholars (not all living at the same time) founded by Ezra about 450 B.C.E. They were largely responsible for the arrangement of the Canon (Bible).

The Men of the Great Synagogue also began the arrangement of the Prayer Book and many of its main prayers. One of their purposes was to counteract the use of the vernacular for prayer and they insisted where possible that Hebrew be the language for prayer. One of the last of these scholars was Simon the Just mentioned in the beginning of Ethics of the Fathers (S.P.B. p. 184).

Kabbalah: קַבָּלָה Tradition. This term has a number of meanings:

(i) A system of Jewish mystical philosophy which has played a very important part in the theological and exegetical literature of both Jews and Christians since the Middle Ages.

(ii) In the Talmud and Midrash, Kabbalah denoted the whole of Jewish tradition then extant.

(iii) The diploma issued to those passing their examination as Shochetim.

Torah: תּוֹרָה Instruction. The Law. In its narrowest sense it applies to the Pentateuch or Five Books of Moses. More commonly it is applied to the whole of the Jewish Religion, both on its practical and on its speculative side.

Shulchan Aruch: שֻׁלְחָן עָרוּךְ Literally, "The Prepared Table." The name given to the famous codification of Jewish law by Rabbi Joseph Karo (16th century).

Ethics

Jewish ethical teaching is found interwoven in the basic sources of Jewish life from the Bible through the Talmud and Rabbinic writings down to the medieval philosophers and legalists. It is a teaching which finds its way into all aspects of the life and thought of man. Many of the Jewish ethical concepts can be really understood only through a knowledge of the Hebrew phrase which is a kind of key phrase or value term to the Jewish ethical lesson. The following are just a few of the most important Jewish ethical terms with their translation.

Ben Adam Lamakom: בֵּין אָדָם לַמָּקוֹם	Those duties which concern the relationship of man to his Maker.
Ben Adam Lachavero: בֵּין אָדָם לַחֲבֵרוֹ	Those duties which concern man's relationship to his fellow as a member of society.
Ben Adam L'atzmo: בֵּין אָדָם לְעַצְמוֹ	Duties of man to himself in fulfilling all his potentialities in life.
Yirat Chet: יִרְאַת חֵטְא	The fear of sin.
Yirat Shamayim: יִרְאַת שָׁמַיִם	The fear of God (lit. heaven).
Teshuvah: תְּשׁוּבָה	Repentance.
Shechinah: שְׁכִינָה	The Divine Presence of which man must be ever aware.
Iyyun Tefillah: עִיּוּן תְּפִלָּה	Devotion in Prayer.
Kavannah: כַּוָּנָה	Concentration and deliberation in performing a sacred task.
Mitzvah: מִצְוָה	A good deed.
Kiddush Hashem: קִדּוּשׁ הַשֵּׁם	The sanctification of God's name. This is eternally the ideal motive for all man's actions.
Chillul Hashem: חִלּוּל הַשֵּׁם	The profanation of the Name. The complete reverse of the above and the real character of sin, particularly for the Jew.
Gemilut Chasadim: גְּמִילוּת חֲסָדִים	The practice of charity; (lit. bestowing acts of kindness).
Hachnasat Orchim: הַכְנָסַת אוֹרְחִים	Hospitality to the wayfarer.

Bikkur Cholim:
בִּקּוּר חוֹלִים

Visiting the sick.

Halvayat Hamet:
הַלְוָיַת הַמֵּת

Participation in funeral rites.

Tzedakah: צְדָקָה

Acts of righteousness. A wide term which applies to any kindly or right social action.

Emet: אֱמֶת

Truth.

Middat Haddin
מִדַּת הַדִּין

The quality of Justice. In Jewish ethical teaching Justice is regarded as a pillar supporting human society. This, rather than the impracticable ethic of love, is the requisite for a world at peace.

Lifnim Mishurat Haddin:
לִפְנִים מִשּׁוּרַת הַדִּין

Beyond the strict line of justice, i.e. to do a little more than the law really requires in acts of kindness.

Middat Harachamim:
מִדַּת הָרַחֲמִים

The quality of mercy. Usually applies to God's attribute of mercy.

Kibbud Av Va'em:
כִּבּוּד אָב וָאֵם

The honour due to parents.

Derech Eretz:
דֶּרֶךְ אֶרֶץ

Good conduct. The words mean literally "the ways of the land," The term indicates the supreme ideal of gentlemanly conduct in all matters affecting our social life. It is one of the most comprehensive Jewish ethical terms

Yetzer Tov:
יֵצֶר טוֹב

The good inclination, i.e. the disposition of the well trained and disciplined character of a virtuous man.

Yetzer Ra:

יֵצֶר רָע

The evil inclination signifying the weakness (usually of the flesh) which in rabbinic psychology stands against the good inclination.

Tz'neeut: צְנִיעוּת   Modesty or chastity.

Anavah: עֲנָוָה   Humility, submissiveness.

THE BASIC SOURCES OF JEWISH
LIFE AND THOUGHT

1. Sources of Jewish Life and Thought

In this section we will take the main development of Jewish teaching through its greater books. These books have in the first place shaped Jewish life but they have also had a considerable influence on world civilisation as a whole.

Although the Bible should really be treated in a class of its own, we include it here for the sake of showing an outline of the continuous development of Jewish thought from its chief source which is the Bible. This survey will not include any Jewish classics of the modern period.

X

The Bible and its Contents

This is known to us by the term תנ״ך (Tanach) a three letter symbol in which each letter stands for one division of the Bible. The ת stands for תורה (Torah) which here includes only the Five Books of Moses or Pentateuch. These are

בְּרֵאשִׁית, שְׁמוֹת, וַיִּקְרָא, בַּמִּדְבָּר, דְּבָרִים.

Genesis, Exodus, Leviticus, Numbers, Deuteronomy.

The נ which is the second letter in the symbol תנ״ך stands for נְבִיאִים (Prophets). This division is first of all divided into two parts which we call נְבִיאִים רִאשׁוֹנִים (Former Prophets) and נְבִיאִים אַחֲרוֹנִים (Latter Prophets).

The נְבִיאִים רִאשׁוֹנִים (Former Prophets) are not really prophetic books at all. They are all chiefly historical books and carry the historical record of Israel from the death of Moses until the Babylonian exile. These are the books of Joshua, Judges, Samuel I and II, Kings I and II.

The נְבִיאִים אַחֲרוֹנִים (Latter Prophets) contain the speeches of the great prophets of Israel. Some of these teachers left us large collections of their speeches which were compiled into rather big books. These we usually call the **Major Prophets.** There are three such major books: Isaiah, Jeremiah and Ezekiel.

In addition there are twelve **Minor Prophets,** so called only because their books are very much smaller. The list is as follows: Hosea, Joel, Amos, Obadiah, Jonah, Micah, Nahum, Habakkuk, Zephaniah, Haggai, Zechariah, Malachi.

The third and last letter, the כ, stands for כְּתוּבִים (Writings). This is a collection of great books made up as follows: Psalms, Proverbs, Job; five Megillot or small scrolls which are Song of Songs, Ruth, Ecclesiastes, Lamentations and Esther; the historical books Daniel, Ezra, Nehemiah, Chronicles I and II.

XI

The Prayer Book

Few people will not readily appreciate the importance of knowing something about the Prayer Book, the book which next to the Bible itself has been the most cherished possession of the Jew and his constant link between him and God. Little do we realise as we handle our Prayer Book in Synagogue and at home that it embodies Jewish prayer stretching over three thousand years and more, and in its devotions for the weekday, Sabbath, festival and personal occasions it embraces the history and philosophy, the life and thought of our people from earliest times, and contains the deep religious expressions of the classical ages of Judaism when the flower of Jewish religious genius was at its best.

Public Prayer

Individual prayer is as old as recorded history and in our Bible we have the record of the prayers of the great men and women of our early story. Thus the Bible tells of the prayers of Abraham and Jacob, of Moses, of Hannah, David and Daniel—simple prayers all of them, expressing in words the outpourings of the soul. But the distinctiveness of Jewish worship lies not in the individual prayer but in congregational worship. This is perhaps the distinguishing aspect of Jewish prayer, the development of congregational or public prayer. Just when it started is difficult to decide but it seems safe enough to say that public worship among the Jews was known in the days of the Prophets during the existence of the first Temple, say in the 7th and 8th centuries B.C.E. This development of public or congregational worship, which later found its fullest expression in the Jewish synagogue, was the particular contribution of Judaism and was in time taken over and used also by Christianity and Mohammedanism. With the importance of public worship there grew up certain traditions later codified into law, which recommended certain prayers for public worship only. These prayers like the Kaddish and the Kedushah which were adopted for Reader and congregational responses quite obviously are intended only for public worship.

Basic Elements

Let us now turn to the liturgy of the Prayer Book and see first of all what were the prayers originally used in the early synagogues. Without doubt the most ancient prayers are certain psalms and the Shema. Together with the congregational responses they were taken over by the early Synagogue directly from the ancient Temple service. The psalms, as we have seen, were often chanted in the Temple as a feature of the Temple worship and it seems reasonable to suppose that when people met for congregational worship in the early Synagogue they used the Psalter as a ready source for their devotional readings. The Shema was long recognised as embodying the cardinal principles of the Jewish faith and all are agreed that the public recitation of the Shema was a regular feature of the original Synagogue as it was in the ritual of the Temple. Further than these parts of the early service, we have no evidence of any other statutory prayers. It was not until the 4th and 3rd centuries B.C.E. that the men of the Great Synagogue, who were constituted as an authoritive assembly for all matters religious, developed the Synagogue service along the more elaborate lines by which it is recognised today. Accepting the sections of the Shema as a central and important declaration of faith they introduced the two introductory paragraphs which precede the Shema. The first speaks of God as the creator of light, the God of Nature; and the second of the place of Torah in the life of the Jew (S.P.B. 39). After the Shema they prescribed a prayer dealing with God the redeemer of Israel (S.P.B. p. 43). They further were responsible for the compilation of the **Shemone Esrei**, the 18 benedictions or the **Amidah,** so called because it is read standing. And finally, they regularised the Torah readings as part of the service on Holy Days, Mondays and Thursdays.

We now have the main essentials of the Service as they were developed by the 3rd century B.C.E., the Shema, the Psalms and the Responses taken over from the Temple and the benedictions preceding and following the Shema, the Amidah and the regular Torah readings which were introduced by the men of the Great Synagogue.

One further point ought to be noticed about the work of the men of the Great Synagogue for they, it seems, were responsible for formulating the statutory times for prayer—morning, afternoon and evening.

XI.—*The Prayer Book*

Thus the fundamentals of our Synagogue service remain the same as they were over two thousand years ago, and what else we have in our Siddur was developed in succeeding ages—chiefly up to the end of the 11th century—after which little, if anything, was added to the statutory service though many hymns were written in the later Middle Ages to find their way into the Jewish Prayer Book to be recited on special days.

There are certain general features of the Siddur which we do well to keep in mind if we wish to gain a true picture of this remarkable book. Perhaps one of the most important characteristics of the Siddur is that it is not only a book of prayer but also an anthology of devotional readings. The fact is that there are several passages in our Siddur which, properly speaking, are not prayers at all. The excerpts from the Talmud and other rabbinic literature or the famous chapters of **Ethics of the Fathers** (p. 184) cannot be regarded as prayers. Nonetheless they have an honoured place in the Jewish Prayer Book because religious study was always an important religious exercise and would often produce a spiritual experience as profound and as satisfying as prayer itself. That is why several passages belonging to this category are to be found in the Siddur.

Another general characteristic of our Prayer Book is that it reflects in its pages a number of primary Jewish religious doctrines including our concept of God, the election of Israel, the divine source of the Torah, the providence of God and our hope for the Messiah. All these and other philosophical religious teachings of Judaism are interwoven into the fabric of our daily prayers to an extent that makes the Siddur an important source book of Jewish religious philosophy. A good example of this can be found in the **Alenu** (p. 76) one of the noblest of our prayers, and one which is associated with the story of Jewish martyrdom. In the first of its two paragraphs we find the idea of Israel's election and in the second paragraph the purpose of this election is joined to a grand universalistic ideal which anticipates the day "when the Lord shall be one and his name one."

Jewish attitudes are reflected also in the preponderance of praises over petitions because the religious spirit is best expressed in a mood of thanksgiving and joyous optimism. Foremost in this group of doxologies are those in which we sing of God's sublimity and holiness. The **Kedushah** (p. 45) is a beautiful responsive song ascribing to God the perfection of holiness. In this class of doxologies we include also the famous **Kaddish**. Originally it was the parting prayer of a teacher after his lesson and then a concluding prayer of the service. In time it became more famous as a prayer recited by mourners. In ascribing greatness and holiness to God the mourner expresses his firm faith in God's goodness and His just ordering of His universe.

These are just a few indications of the majesty of our Siddur which make it one of the basic sources of Jewish life and thought.

XII

The Talmud

It is usual to say that the Jews possess two Laws. The first is the Written Law or תּוֹרָה שֶׁבִּכְתָב; the second is the Oral Law or תּוֹרָה שֶׁבְּעַל פֶּה. Now the Written Law is quite clearly the Bible whose different sections we have just listed. The Oral Law is more difficult to explain but it represents one of the most important features of Jewish life and thought throughout the ages. Briefly, we might say that the Oral Law is the great body of Jewish teaching, tradition and biblical interpretation, all of which was handed down orally by teacher to pupil, by father to son, throughout the ages, from the earliest days of Israel's history until our own day.

Now the term Oral Law suggests that it was never written down. The Talmud however represents a new stage in the transmission of the Oral Law by having it all put down in writing.

The Mishnah

The real story begins with the destruction of the Second Jewish Commonwealth and Temple in the year 70 C.E. At that time there lived a great rabbi named **Jochanan Ben Zakkai** who did much to spread the idea that it was not impossible for Jews to live without a country of their own and without a Temple. In their place he made the practice of Judaism central. Due to his work and to the rabbis who followed, many schools were established in Palestine and elsewhere and Judaism was carefully taught and discussed. Everywhere there was Jewish study and an eagerness and love for Jewish learning. By this time there were collections or little books of accepted rabbinic teachings and traditions and about the year 200 C.E. one of the greatest rabbis of a great age—**Rabbi Judah The Prince**—collected them all and edited them, compiling them into one authoritative work which we call the **Mishnah.**

The **Mishnah** is thus the collection of Jewish tradition and teaching which was originally handed down from earliest days in an oral form but was finally compiled into a written collection by **Judah The Prince** about the year 200 C.E.

It is divided into six orders, sometimes called **Shass** from the Hebrew letters שׁס which are the abbreviations of the words שִׁשָׁה סְדָרִים (six orders). They are: (1) זְרָעִים (**Seeds**) which deal mainly with the agricultural laws of Israel. (2) מוֹעֵד (**Festival**) dealing with matters related to the Sabbath and festivals. (3) נָשִׁים (**Women**) containing the laws connected chiefly with marriage and divorce. (4) נְזִיקִין (**Damages**) on Civil and Criminal Law. (5) קָדָשִׁים (**Holy Things**) dealing with the laws of sacrifice and Temple ritual. (6) טָהֳרוֹת (**Purification**) which contains chiefly laws dealing with personal and religious purity.

The **Mishnah** represents the written codification of rabbinic collections up to the end of the 2nd century of the present era and contains the views of about 120 teachers. The teacher in the **Mishnah** is called a **Tanna** (lit. to teach by repetition. The meaning is the same as the word **Shanah** from which we get **Mishnah**).

The Gemara

When the Mishnah was complete, the later scholars subjected each paragraph to detailed discussions and thorough examination. These later scholars are known as **Amoraim** (speakers) and their lengthy discussions are what is called the **Gemara** (supplement or completion). The **Gemara** is not confined to the scholarly discussion on the **Mishnah** although that is its chief purpose. In fact, it embraces all kinds of subjects ranging over history, legend, ethics, science and many other interesting discussions that were debated in the rabbinic schools.

The **Mishnah** and **Gemara** together are known as the **Talmud**. Since there were academies of learning in Palestine and in Babylon there were two kinds of Talmud. The Palestinian Talmud was left unfinished. The Babylonian Talmud which is the more authoritative and the one generally studied was finished about 500. It is one of the world's greatest books and next to the Bible has influenced Jewish life and thought more than anything else.

XIII

The Midrash

The word **Midrash** means "Inquiry" and is the general term applied to a large and very important section of Jewish literature.

Right from the time the Jews began to read the Bible an attempt was made to explain the text in as many ways as seemed possible to the inquiring mind of the Jewish teachers and scholars. The **Midrash** is the result of such Biblical interpretation which seeks to go below the surface of the text and arrive at its spirit. The **Midrash** contains a wealth of moral teachings, legends and parables, and much of it represents a kind of popular homiletics or short sermon outlines. But not all of it is of that character for some parts of the **Midrash** are legal in spirit and very close to the legal parts of the **Talmud** in content.

Such a vast work which covers the rabbinic interpretation of the whole of the Bible does not belong to one age. In fact the earlier parts were in existence before the books of the Bible were finally set in their present order, while the later parts of the **Midrash** are as late as the 10th or 11th centuries of the present era.

The greatness and the eternal value of the **Midrash** lies in its Haggadah, i.e. the ethical teachings which the rabbis sought to impress upon their readers. Unlike the Halachah or legal discussions and pronouncements, the Haggadah is more interested in ideas than in details. The Haggadic literature represents in miniature the religious genius of the Jewish people. Here we find sublime ethics and philosophic wisdom, as well as a vast amount of folklore. Written in a popular and impressive style it drew the hearts of the people who found in it a deep source of spiritual comfort and moral strength.

In addition, the **Midrash-Haggadah** became a powerful means of educating the people to see the significance and beauty of Judaism. It is true, of course, that a considerable amount of this Haggadic literature is found interwoven in the pages of the Talmud, but primarily the Haggadah is the crowning feature of the **Midrash**.

The most important Midrashim are known as follows: **Midrash Rabbah** on the entire Pentateuch and the five Megillot, **Mechiltah** on Exodus, **Sifra** on Leviticus, **Sifre** on Numbers, **Mechiltah** on Deuteronomy, **Pesikta** on the festivals and special days and **Tanchuma** on the entire Pentateuch.

XIV

Medieval Scholars and Writers

Rashi

Of all the medieval Jewish commentators of the Bible and Talmud the greatest is **Rashi** (abbreviated from Rabbi Solomon b. Isaac 1040-1105). His commentary on the Talmud is remarkable in explaining the meaning of the text and making it intelligible even to a beginner. The commentary on the Bible relies on authorities such as the Midrash and Talmud which Rashi quotes to illustrate the text. Through the fame of Rashi, France took the lead in Talmudic scholarship and his influence among succeeding students was carried on and even increased. To this day no real student of Bible or Talmud would study the Hebrew text without Rashi's commentary.

If France was noted for its Talmudical scholarship, Spain became famous for its Jewish philosophy and poetry.

In this section we can only list the most outstanding Jewish classics which have influenced Jewish life and thought and it will be more convenient to refer to them under the heading of their authors. The first and the last of our list do not belong to the Spanish period.

Saadiah (892-942)

Born in Egypt he was the forerunner of many later Jewish philosophers who were influenced by his work. Among his numerous works we must mention his Arabic translation of the Scripture, a commentary on the mystical "Book of Creation" of unknown authorship in which he expounded his doctrine of the creation and his view of the universe. But most important of all, and the work which makes Saadiah famous for all time is his **Emunot Vedeot** (Beliefs and Opinions) a philosophical exposition of Judaism. For the first time, Judaism was explained philosophically and an attempt was made to bring religious belief and opinion into harmony with the current Greek philosophical doctrines. This was a task continued by other writers who followed Saadiah.

XIV.—*Medieval Scholars and Writers*

Solomon Ibn Gabirol (1021-1070)

Our first name in the great Spanish-Jewish period. His claim to fame lies in his ability as a poet and philosopher. His two greatest works are **Keter Malchut** (The Kingly Crown) which is a glorious series of poems about God and the world in which the poet pours out his heart unreservedly to his Creator. The second is his **Mekor Chayim** (Fountain of Life) which is a philosophical work that did much to introduce certain aspects of Greek philosophy to the western world. Until the middle of the 19th century this work was known only in its Latin version, Fons Vitae, and was assigned to an author named Avicebron.

Yehuda Halevi (1085-1140)

Was one of the brightest stars of the great Spanish-Jewish period. His fame rests in the first place on his reputation as the writer of beautiful Hebrew poems among which the most famous are his **Odes to Zion.** Many of his poems have found their way into the liturgy. Another work that must be noted is Halevi's **Kuzari,** a philosophical dialogue between the King of the Khazars and a Rabbi, in the course of which the beliefs of the Jew and the teachings of Judaism are explained. Halevi made the attempt to free Jewish thought from sub-servience to Arab and Greek philosophy. Generally speaking, he was the exponent of faith rather than reason as the basis for religion.

Moses Maimonides (1135-1204)

The greatest Jewish scholar of the Middle Ages, Maimonides left his permanent impression on Jewish thought. His two most important works were (*a*) **Mishneh Torah** or **Yad Hachazakah**—the Strong Hand, which is a masterly compilation of Jewish law in fourteen volumes, clearly arranged and lucidly expounded. It is a veritable encyclopedia of Jewish rabbinic law. (*b*) **The Guide to the Perplexed** or **Moreh Nevuchim** is a philosophical treatment of Jewish thought. Aristotelian philosophy had gained a place of prominence during the Middle Ages and Maimonides attempts to reconcile Aristotle's teachings with that of the Bible and Judaism.

The Shulchan Aruch

This work means, literally, "The Table Prepared" and was written by Rabbi **Joseph Karo** (born in Spain in 1488 and died in Safed in 1575). His masterpiece is an orderly and comprehensive compilation of the whole of Jewish law as it was developed by the 16th century. It finalised the divergencies of opinion by creating a standard and authorised norm of Jewish religious behaviour. The Shulchan Aruch gained the immediate attention of the Jewish world and together with the notes of **Isserles** (1520-1572) it became the established code also for Ashkenazi Jews. To this day it still represents the climax of orthodox Judaism which establishes the lines of Jewish religious conduct in conformity with its principles.

HEBREW

XV

The Alphabet

The letters of the Hebrew Alphabet were perhaps originally shaped to represent the objects denoted by their names thus the **Ayin** (which means "eye") was written o and the letter **Shin** (tooth) was written W.

There are 22 letters all consonants and 10 vowels, five long and five short.

There are a number of ways of writing the Alphabet, as follows:

A. Ordinary square form characters: Known as כְּתָב אַשּׁוּרִית (Assyrian) this is the most popular form now used for printing Hebrew.

B. Script or cursive form: Used in writing. It is of German origin.

C. Alternative script form.

D. Rabbinic form: Used by Talmudic commentators and scholars. It is known as the "Rashi" script. Rashi was the pen name of the renowned French Bible and Talmud commentator (1040-1105).

E. Torah Script: Used for scrolls of the Bible, Mezuzah, Tephillin.

Note: In the Torah script the 7 letters שׁ ע׳ ט׳ נ׳ ז׳ ג׳ץ have three short strokes above them known as **Taggin.**

The 6 letters ד׳ ב׳ ק ח׳ י׳ ה have one stroke (besides the stroke which forms part of the letter itself).

(*a*) The letter ח is written so ﬡ in the Pentateuch and Mezuzah (i.e. the letter ו written twice, attached on top).

(*b*) In Tephillin the letter ח is written so ﬡ consisting of a ו and a ז attached on top.

67

Name	A	B	C	D	E	Sound in Ash-kenazi Hebrew	Num-erical Value	Final Forms §§
Alef	א	lc	א	ɓ	א	Silent	I	
Bet	בּ }	ג	בּ	ʒ	ڊ	{ B	2	
Vet	ב }					V		
Gimel	ג	ڂ	ג	ג	אל	G	3	
Dalet	ד	ʔ	ד	ד	ד	D	4	
Hay	ה	ה	ה	ה	הי	H	5	
Vav	ו	ı	ו	ו	ו	V	6	
Zayin	ז	ל	ך	ɜ	ז	Z	7	
Chet	ח	ח	ח	ם	חש	CH	8	
Tet	ט	G	ט	ע	ש	T	9	
Yud	י	ı	י	י	צ	Y	IO	
Kaf	כּ }	כק	ך	ד י	רל	{ K	20	ך §§
Chaf	כל }					CH		
Lamed	ל	ʃ	ל	ל	ל	L	30	
Mem	מ	מ פ	ם מ	ם ח	ממ	M	40	ם §§
Nun	נ	נ	נ ו	ם כ	נל	N	50	ן §§
Samech	ס	o	ס	ﻣ	ע	S	60	
Ayin	ע	צ	ע	ע	ע	Silent	70	
Pay	פּ }	פ	ף פ	ף פ	פ	{ P	80	ף §§
Fay	פ }					F		
Tzadi	צ	ʒ	צ ץ	ץ	צ	TZ	90	ץ §§
Kuf	ק	ק	ק	ק	ק	K	IOO	
Resh	ר	ר	ר	ר	ר	R	200	
Shin	שׁ }	ℓ	ש	ﺳ	ש	{ Sh	300	
Sin	שׂ }					S		
Tav	תּ }	ת	ת	ת	ת	{ T	400	
Sav	ת }					S *		

* In Modern Hebrew the ת is sounded as T

XV.—The Alphabet

Vowels

Sign	Name	Sound	Sign	Name	Sound
	Long	**Vowels**		**Short**	**Vowels**
ָ	Komatz	A in far	—	Patoch	A in bat
ֵ	Ts'ere	AI in mail	ֶ	Segol	E in get
ִ	Chirrik	EA in sea	ִ	Chirrek	I in bit
וֹ	Cholom	O in come	ָ	Komotz	O in got
וּ	Shuruk	U in flute	ֻ	Kubutz	U in put
ָ	Komatz	O in come	—	Patoch	A in bat
ֵ	Ts'ere	AI in mail	ֶ	Segol	E in get
ִ	Chirrik	EA in sea	ִ	Chirrek	I in bit
וֹ	Cholom	OA in coat	ָ	Komotz	O in got
וּ	Shuruk	U in flute	ֻ	Kubutz	U in put

SEPHARDI

ASHKENAZI

The sign : (Sheva) indicates the absence of a vowel. When sounded has a very short sound, as the E in RE-CEIVE.

The Neginot

1. Introduction: By Neginot we mean all those small strokes, signs, dots or peculiar characters which are generally to be found below, above, at the beginning or at the end of Hebrew words in the Bible. These strokes or accents as they are sometimes called, must not be confused with the vowels. They are called Neginot from the Hebrew word נגן which means "to play an instrument" or "to sing" or "to chant."

2. Their purpose in Hebrew Grammar: In Hebrew Grammar the Neginot (also called cantillations or disjunctive and conjunctive accents) are very important since they are an aid to a better understanding of the text. Their purpose is often to indicate the position of the stress or accent in words and to serve as punctuation marks, showing the natural pauses in the sentence.

3. Their Musical Purpose:

Their usual significance is recognised as a guide to the chanting of the sacred text. There are some 24 different notes used in chanting the Hebrew text. There are three different systems in use at the present time.

(*a*)   Those used for chanting the text of the Torah (Pentateuch).

(*b*)   Those used for chanting the text of the Haftarah (i.e. all the Biblical books except the Psalms, Proverbs, Job).

(*c*)   Those used for chanting the three books of the Bible, Psalms, Proverbs, Job.

These three books are usually called אֱ מֶ' ת from the three initial letters of the words:

Job	אִיוֹב
Proverbs	מִשְׁלֵי
Psalms	תְּהִלִּים

and their Neginot are called טַעֲמֵי אֱמֶת.

Each of these signs has an Aramaic name and the name usually helps us to understand the way in which the "note" is to be sounded.

Hebrew Name	Pronounced	Position	Shape
מַהְפַּךְ	Mahpach	below	<
פַּשְׁטָא	Pashtah	above	ר
זָקֵף־קָטָן	Zakayf-katon	above	:
זָקֵף־גָּדוֹל	Zakayf-gadol	above	־:
מֵרְכָה	May-rechah	below	
טִפְּחָא	Tip-chah	below	
מוּנַח	Munach	below	־ا
אֶתְנַחְתָּא	Et-nach-tah	below	ה
דַּרְגָּא	Dar-gah	below	S
תְּבִיר	Tevir	below	ر
קַדְמָא	Kadmah	above	ر
אַזְלָא	Azlah	above	(
גֵּרֵשׁ	Geresh	above	
גֵּרְשַׁיִם	Gayr-shayyim	above	((
תְּלִישָׁא־קְטַנָּה	Tleeshah-ketanah	above	ه
תְּלִישָׁא־גְדוֹלָה	Tleeshah-gedolah	above	؟
פָּזֵר	Pa-zayr	above	۷
רְבִיעַ	Re-vee-ah	above	.
סֶגּוֹל	Seggol	above	∴
זַרְקָא	Zarkah	above	ه
יְתִיב	Yetiv	below	<ا
סִלּוּק	Seeluk	below	ا
סוֹף־פָּסוּק	Soff-pasuk	below	۱
שַׁלְשֶׁלֶת	Shal-shellet	above	ξ

There are one or two other accents which occur very rarely.

HISTORY

XVI

A Bird's Eye View of Jewish History

Abraham to the Present Day

Introduction: Jewish History is a wonderful and exciting story of a people scattered throughout many lands over thousands of years. Except to the select few it is not likely that the whole story of the Jewish people will be known. This is understandable, bearing in mind the complicated nature of the story.

For this reason it is felt that a short guide can serve a useful purpose to the average layman. Its purpose is to present the reader with an idea of the main sequence of events, of general trends in Jewish history, and to indicate by chapter headings where he might enquire further into periods that hold greater interest for him.

CHAPTER ONE

The First Jewish Commonwealth
2000 B.C.E.—586 B.C.E.

The Early Beginnings of the Hebrew Tribe—2000 B.C.E.

Our people had a simple beginning. Starting as a small family tribe under the leadership of Abraham, the Hebrew tribe, as it was called, was kept together by a firm belief in One God. This, and the principle of the Brotherhood of Man, were later recognised as the basic principles of the Jewish Religion. Abraham's leadership was passed on after his death to Isaac, who was in turn succeeded by Jacob.

The Sojourn in Egypt—1700 B.C.E.

Towards the last part of Jacob's life, the Hebrew tribe settled in Egypt where in the course of time, they grew so numerous and prosperous that they excited the enmity of a new nationalist dynasty of Egyptian rulers. They were cruelly enslaved by the Pharaohs for a long period of over two hundred years until they were redeemed from the Egyptian slavery by the great leader and prophet—Moses.

The Factors which made us a People

But freedom was only the first step. The Israelites who marched out of Egypt were still slaves in mind. The turbulent and revolutionary murmurings against authority proved that they were not fit yet as a people, and it took forty years in the wilderness before a new generation of courageous men and women were ready for national independence. It was the giving of the Torah which marked the greatest stage in the shaping of a well ordered and disciplined people. It presented them with a national and ideal way of life. They were now ready to embark upon the third stage of their development—entering into a land which would be their own.

Settlement in Canaan

The Israelites conquered territory east of the Jordan before Moses died. His successor, the soldier Joshua, led his people over the Jordan and after taking Jericho they invaded the hill country and strove bitterly with the local tribes before gaining mastery of the land. The country was then parcelled out to the different tribes of Israel for settlement.

The Period of the Judges—1100 B.C.E.

The local tribes were never decisively defeated and they continued to live with and around the Israelites. This presented two great dangers to the Israelites—danger of attack, and the danger of assimilation. The great enemies of the time were mainly the Canaanites, Midianites, Ammonites, and the Philistines and from time to time there arose among the Israelites courageous men (one famous woman) who rallied the people and led them against their enemies. Among such leaders (Shofetim or Judges) were Deborah, Gideon, Jephtha, and Samson. The last and most famous Judge was the "seer" Samuel. He brought a spirit of unity among the people by strengthening their faith and uniting them in the worship of the One God.

The Period of the First Kings—1030 B.C.E.

(*a*)   **Saul.** Towards the end of Samuel's period of office he was persuaded by the people to set a king over them. The choice fell on Saul who was acclaimed the first king of Israel. At first successful, he

later became estranged from Samuel and became subject to melan-
cholia. Saul was finally vanquished by the Philistines and David
became the second king of Israel.

(*b*) **David.** David was the greatest of Israel's kings. He brought
the tribes into a firm union, took Jerusalem from the Jebusites and
established it as his capital. He smote all his enemies in and around
Palestine and left an empire to his son and successor, Solomon.
Besides being a great ruler he was also a great poet and man of God.
He is traditionally the author of a large number of the Psalms.

(*c*) **Solomon**—970 B.C.E. One of Solomon's first tasks was to
erect the magnificent Temple of God. Most of his reign was characterised by peace and prosperity, Solomon reaping the profits of his
father's greatness. But though tradition has built him up as a wise
man, he committed a grave political error in his foreign alliances
which resulted in the introduction into Canaan of idol worship.
Again, in order to erect his extensive and luxurious buildings the
people were severely taxed. On his death, the seeds of his folly yielded
an evil harvest.

The Divided Kingdom—930 B.C.E.

On the death of Solomon the spirit of enmity which already existed
between the north and the south was brought to a climax through the
further folly of Solomon's heir. The people were then divided, the
Kingdom of Israel in the north comprising the revolutionary ten
tribes, and the Kingdom of Judah in the south comprising just the two
tribes of Judah and Benjamin who remained loyal to the dynasty of
David. The two kingdoms were for the greater part bitter rivals and
enemies. In addition, religious, social and political corruption were
characteristic of both kingdoms. It was clear that they could not last.

The Prophets

To fight against the prevalent evil, the prophets fearlessly preached
the message of truth. Elijah, Elisha, Amos, Hosea, Isaiah, Micah and
Jeremiah are among the immortal teachers of mankind. Their strong
message with its underlying spiritual force has been one of the great
Jewish contributions to the world.

Decline and Fall—586 B.C.E.

This period saw the rise of Syria and the great empires of Assyria and
Babylon. The Northern Kingdom of Israel succumbed before the

might of Assyria in 721 B.C.E. and the ten tribes were dispersed. The kingdom of Judah continued under more sober leadership for about a century and a half before it eventually fell under the great military power of Babylon in 586 B.C.E. The Temple was laid in ruins and the better part of the nation exiled to Babylon.

CHAPTER TWO

The Second Jewish Commonwealth
530 B.C.E.—70 C.E.

By the Waters of Babylon—The Return—530 B.C.E.

The exiles in Babylon settled down as best they could in their strange land. There were many however who mourned for Zion and remembered Jerusalem above their chiefest joy. In 539 B.C.E. Cyrus of Persia overthrew the Babylonian empire, and allowed those who wished, to return. The returning exiles were "like unto them that dream" and overcoming many obstacles, particularly from the Samaritans (tribes who were settled in Samaria after the fall of the Northern Kingdom) they reconstructed their national life and erected a new Temple.

Ezra and Nehemiah—450 B.C.E.

But the little community soon floundered before the withering menace of assimilation. Ezra the scribe, and later Nehemiah joined the returned exiles and due to their efforts the people once more were moulded into a strong community devoted to the service of their God. Ezra was responsible for the religious revival among his people, while Nehemiah attended to the work of strengthening the cities to withstand attack. The reforms of Ezra and Nehemiah were followed by a long period of peace and quiet. Hardly affected by the comings and goings of great empires the Jews organised around their Synagogues and led by the Scribes and the Men of the Great Synagogue, they settled down to a period of literary activity which is probably one of the most formative in Jewish history.

Under Greek Rule

Their peace was finally disturbed by the appearance of a world conqueror and Judea in its turn submitted to the rule of Alexander the Great. It was while they lived under Greek influence that the rise of the Hellenistic cult threatened Jewish life as no other civilisation had done before. The rich and the opportunists forsook the paths of their civilisation for what seemed to be the brighter and more profitable way of life of the Greeks. After Alexander's death the tiny Jewish state was the prize for which the rival Syrian and Egyptian generals waged war for over a century before it finally came under Antiochus of Syria.

The Epic Struggle of the Maccabees—165 B.C.E.

Antiochus now began ruthlessly to crush any sign of independence among the Jews. But when he attempted to force a heathen religion upon them the Jews, led by the famous Maccabees, raised the banner of revolt and waged guerilla warfare against an enemy immeasurably stronger than their own ill-armed, ill-trained band. This is the first recorded struggle for religious independence. But the fight against Antiochus was also something of a civil war for the Hellenistic cult had made great inroads into Jewish life and between the Hellenists and the loyal Pietists there was bitter enmity. After a protracted struggle the forces of Antiochus were defeated but it was not until about 140 B.C.E. that Simon the sole survivor of the Maccabean brothers was made High Priest and Prince of the nation, and Rome, the supreme power of the time, recognised the independence of Judea. The rule of the Maccabees continued for about a century when in 63 B.C.E. Pompey intervened in a fratricidal struggle, took Jerusalem and brought the people to a state of submission to all-powerful Rome.

Under Roman Rule—70 C.E.

The Jews did not easily bear the Roman yoke. Procurators followed one another and vied with each other in their brutality towards the Judeans who were again divided among themselves; the Zealots of Galilee dreamed of independence, the Essenes dreamed of the Messiah, while the nobles curried favour with the Roman rulers.

The Rise of Christianity

About this time the teachings of Jesus of Nazareth obtained a following among certain Jews, particularly in Galilee. Jesus did not teach the abrogation of the Torah and most of his teaching is good Jewish ethics. His disciples regarded him as the Messiah or king and he was accused to the Roman governor, Pontius Pilate, as being a menace to law and order. Jesus was crucified by the Romans but his teaching was spread by his followers and due mainly to Paul the members of the new sect broke from Judaism and developed an entirely new religion.

The Destruction of the Second Temple

The real struggle with Rome began about 65 C.E., when the Zealots organised open warfare against Rome. The struggle was heroic but unequal and in 70 C.E. Titus captured Jerusalem and burned the Temple. Thus ended the second Jewish State and from that point began the great Jewish exile.

CHAPTER THREE

The Period of the Rabbis
70—1000 C.E.

Jochanan Ben Zakkai saves Jewish Life

While the battering rams of the Romans were still breaking against the walls of Jerusalem, the far-sighted action of the rabbi who saved from destruction the centre of Jewish learning, laid the foundations of a new sort of life which was to keep the Jews as a distinctive entity. Without a Temple, land or idependence, scattered throughout many centres, the Jews found their unifying principle in the Torah and its study. For more than three centuries the rabbinical Patriarchs were the recognised authorities of the Jewish world. It was a period of religious reconstruction and intense intellectual activity. The Synagogue and Prayer Book took the place of the Temple and sacrifice. Learning was widespread and child education almost universal among the Jews.

The Revolt of Bar Kochba—132—135 C.E.

The smouldering fires of hatred against the Romans were soon stirred up once again into a roaring flame, and the Jewish army rallied behind Bar Kochba in an attempt to throw off the Roman yoke. The heroic struggle received the support of Rabbi Akiva, the greatest Tanna, or teacher, of the century. At first successful, the Jewish army soon had to face the strong forces of Julius Severus, and one by one the Jewish points of resistance were broken down. After the fall of Bethar, the Emperor Hadrian imposed cruel restrictions on the Palestine Jewish community, and many more left their homeland for safer abodes elsewhere. The successors of Hadrian relaxed some of the laws and for a time the scholars of Palestine were left in comparative peace to continue the development of the Talmud.

Life in Palestine

About the year 200, Rabbi Judah the Prince edited the Mishnah, the great body of oral law developed by the Tannaim. For more than two centuries after this the Palestinian community continued to exist and the Palestinian Talmud and Midrash was the result of the labours of these rabbis.

Gradually the rift between Judaism and Christianity grew wider and when Christianity was adopted by Constantine as the official state religion (312), the position of the Jews in Palestine grew intolerable. The power of the Patriarchs declined and the office was finally abolished in 425.

The Jews in Babylon

Well before the destruction of the Temple in 70 C.E., settlements of Jews had already appeared in Alexandria, Arabia, Asia Minor, and in some of the Mediterranean islands. The most important Jewish community however was to be found in Babylon which assumed its place of pre-eminence in Jewish life not long after the decline of Palestinian Jewry. The people possessed a large measure of autonomy, and were exceedingly well organised. The Exilarch, or Prince of the Exile, was the recognised head of the people. The academies of Sura, Pumbeditha, Mehozah and Nehardea were crowded to overflowing and Jewish scholarship flourished. The great work of the Babylonian Talmud was completed about 500 C.E. In post-Talmudic years the heads of schools were called Geonim (Gaon-Excellency) and in them was vested the religious authority not only of the Jews in Babylon but even outside, since they became the religious guides for Jews all over the diaspora.

The Talmud

The Talmud represents the record of the development of Jewish life and thought through the Mishnah and Gemara, and its six orders cover every aspect of the Jewish civilisation. The Talmud has, more than any other single factor, been the most formative influence on Jewish life.

The End of the Talmudic Period

By the beginning of the 7th century a new force had thrown down its challenge to the world. The conquering sword of the Mohammedans swept through the Byzantine empire taking Palestine, and wresting Babylon from its Persian rulers. At first their rule was that of "The Koran or the Sword" but in the course of time their fanatical zeal was abated and they became satisfied with the tribute and homage of the unbelievers. By this time Jewish life in Babylon was fast declining, and the great splendour of the Exilarch and Geonim became but a mere shadow. The rift caused by the Karaite sect—opponents of rabbinic authority—hastened the time when Babylon ceased to be the chief Jewish settlement. The twilight continued for a time until the academies and Geonim ceased to function in 1038 C.E.

Another country had now established for itself a place of pre-eminence in Jewish life.

CHAPTER FOUR

The Golden Age in Spain

1000—1500

Spain Conquered by the Arabs

In 711, the Arabs crossed the straits of Gibraltar and conquered Spain. For the next four centuries Spain was the one bright star in a world darkened by the shadows of persecution. The Moors and the Jews had much in common and in the kind atmosphere that prevailed, the march of the giant philosophers, poets, statesmen and scientists created the most brilliant episode in the sombre annals of Galut history.

The March of the Giants

(*a*) **Hasdai Ibn Shaprut** By the 10th century, Jewish roots had struck deep in the soil of Spain. Hasdai was a minister of the Caliph, a patron of learning and a physician of note. His remarkable correspondence with Joseph, king of the Jewish state of Khazars, discovered on the shores of the Caspian Sea, brought a ray of hope into the hearts of the Jews the world over.

(*b*) **Samuel the Prince** He became a chief Minister of the Caliph, and was also a poet and a notable Talmud scholar.

(c) **Solomon Ibn Gabirol** One of the greatest figures of a great age. As a poet and philosopher his fame spread throughout the land and his poems are still included in the Synagogue ritual. In its Latin translation one of his works was used for many years by Christian theologians.

(d) **Bachya Ibn Pakuda** A great philosopher and moralist. His work "The Duties of the Heart" is still a recognised text book of Jewish ethics.

(e) **Yehuda Halevi** "The poet laureate" of the Jews. He sang passionate songs of Zion, and risked his life to set foot on the sacred soil. Many of his poems are included in the Synagogue liturgy.

(f) **Moses Maimonides** He was the most illustrious figure of them all. His fame as a physician was exceeded by his fame as a philosopher. His "Guide to the Perplexed" and "Mishnah Torah" are his greatest works. The "Guide" attempts to reconcile religion with science and it was the cause of a great controversy which bitterly raged throughout the Jewish world.

(g) **Some other great names** Among a host of others it is difficult to single out for special reference any particular name. But mention must be made of the poet Moses Ibn Ezra, the philosopher Abraham Ibn Ezra, and the traveller Benjamin of Tudela.

The Turning Point

Towards the end of the 14th century the Christians had taken all Spain with the exception of Granada.

1391 is the black year since from this point persecution mounted against the Jews in raging fury. Destruction of property, forced baptism and death was the lot of the Jew. Under the leadership of the fanatic Torquemada, the Inquisition rose to its highest point of efficiency, with its fury mainly directed against the Marranos or secret Jews who outwardly professed Catholicism but quietly kept the traditions of their ancestors in the seclusion of their homes.

Expulsion

Torquemada was intent on driving out all the Jews from Spain, and despite the plea of the noble Jewish statesman, Abarbanel, the rulers of Spain were persuaded to follow the counsels of the arch inquisitor. About 200,000 Jews were driven from the shores of Spain on August 2nd, 1492. In that same month Christopher Columbus set out over the uncharted Atlantic.

CHAPTER FIVE

Through the Darkness of Medieval Central Europe
1000—1700

The General Picture

By the beginning of the 11th century Jewish communities were to be found in most European countries. But the picture of medieval European Jewry is one of unbroken gloom. Unable to own land, and barred from the guilds, they were driven to commerce and forced into money lending. In this way some Jews exercised a considerable but unenviable influence in finance.

In cultural affairs the Jews narrowed themselves down to the study of their sacred books, especially the Talmud, and repudiated any attempt to widen their intellectual interests in non-Jewish matters.

Constituting a strange element within the countries of their adoption they were suffered only as a matter of political expediency, and moved about like pawns from one sphere of influence to another, they were subject to most brutal treatment by their Christian oppressors.

The Crusades

The misery of the Jews reached new heights during the period of the Crusades. In 1096, the first Crusade set out to regain Palestine from the Moslems. On their way the Crusaders dealt with the Jewish unbelievers. When faced with the alternative—baptism or death— whole communities perished with the cry of "Shema" on their lips. When this spate of violence died down in its ferocity, the Jew remained subject to numerous restrictive and degrading laws. To escape the hostility shown by the outside world, the Jews huddled together in their ghettos for warmth. Here they developed their inner life, and in their narrow streets and small synagogues they regained their composure together with a sense of dignity and pride in their heritage as Jews.

A Glance into some Countries

(a) **England.** A Jewish community existed in England in the time of William the Conqueror and was fairly treated until 1189 when Richard the Lion Heart was crowned king. Then a wave of persecution broke out and the position steadily deteriorated until the Jews were expelled in 1290.

(b) **Germany.** Jewish communities in Germany bought their freedom and paid dearly for the privilege of being left alone. The illustrious Rabbi Meir of Rothenburg was imprisoned and died there refusing to allow his kinsmen to ransom him. When the Black Death took its heavy toll of life, the accusation was made that the Jews had poisoned the wells and this produced the usual spate of pogroms.

(c) **France.** The general position here was not different from that in other countries in Central Europe. The great Rashi (1040-1105) lived in France and his famous commentary is still a basic subject in the Jewish educational curriculum.

(d) **Italy.** Here the Jews fared much better, and many exiles from Spain found refuge in this country. Italy was so divided politically that in times of stress Jews of one state could find refuge in another. Jewish scholarship flourished due to the activities of the Hebrew printing press.

(e) **Turkish Empire.** In the Turkish Empire Jews lived in comparative freedom, with Constantinople and Salonika as their two great centres. Joseph the Jewish Duke of Naxos tried unsuccessfully to restore Jews to Palestine.

(f) **Holland.** Holland became in the latter Middle Ages a great centre of Jewish life and learning, and Amsterdam became a "new Jerusalem." Manasseh Ben Israel was instrumental in securing the return of the Jews to England. Baruch Spinoza, the famous Jewish thinker, was excommunicated by the Community for his philosophical teachings which the Jews and Christians considered heretical.

False Messiahs

Stirred by Cabbalistic mysticism and motivated by a deep yearning for redemption, the background was set for a strange group of false leaders who claimed divine authority. These false messiahs claimed to be the appointed leaders of God who would bring an end to the sufferings of the Jews and lead the nation back to Palestine. Among them were David Reubeni and Solomon Molcho. The most fantastic of them all was Sabbatai Zevi (1650). The false messiahs attracted large followings in many lands because the people thirsted for a ray of hope to shine out of the unrelieved darkness. All the more poignant was their disappointment when their simple hope was dashed to the ground.

XVI.—*The Great Centres of Poland and Russia*

The Ghetto Walls Stand Strong

Through the long period of the Middle Ages the Jews in darkest Europe lived only to strengthen their inner life. When the Ghetto walls finally broke, they were dazzled by the strange light of an unknown world.

CHAPTER SIX

The Great Centres of Poland and Russia

1500—1900

Early Tolerance

By the middle of the 16th century, Polish Jewry was the largest and most important Jewish community. They were kindly treated and allowed to practice any trade and even to farm land. In their turn, the Jews provided a much needed middle class for the Polish economy and the rules of the country protected them whenever their rights were in danger.

Self Government

The Jews achieved a large measure of autonomy. Each community elected its representatives who sat on the supreme Jewish "Council of the Four Lands." This Council met to decide on all matters affecting Jewish life in Poland, religious, legal, civil and particularly educational.

The Chmielnicki Massacres—1648

The peace was brought to an end when the Cossacks attacked the lords and nobles of the land. At the same time they vented their fury on the Jews whom they considered the tools of the landed classes, and from this point the lot of the Polish Jews was one of intense persecution. As a result, many of them, in their desperation, turned to the false messiahs, Sabbatai Zevi and Jacob Frank.

Chassidism

This was a "revolution" led by Israel Baal Shem, against the dry-as-dust bookishness of Talmud Judaism. The Baal Shem shifted the emphasis from scholarship to piety, from the Talmud to the Prayer Book. He preached that one must serve God in joy. This new message opened up a wonderful source of life for the masses of the ordinary people, unlearned in Talmud, who sought to come near to their God in new ways.

The movement introduced a spirit of freshness and joy, of faith and new life into the hearts of countless numbers. The strong opposition put by the Mitnagdim opponents under their leader the Gaon of Vilna, led to much trouble. But Chassidism captured the imagination of Polish Jewry and did much to strengthen their religious feeling.

Russia Takes Over

Between 1772-1796, the state of chaos in Poland led her ravenous neighbours to annex large parts of Polish territory. Russia took for herself White Russia, Lithuania and the Ukraine, together with over a million Jews who lived in these districts.

Not knowing how to deal with her new Jewish subjects, the first reaction was to prevent the Jews from entering Russia proper. Later, various experiments were attempted to Russianise the Jews, and to accelerate the process Nicholas I introduced his "catchers" to kidnap an annual quota of Jewish youngsters for the army. Here many of them were cruelly treated in the attempt to make them accept baptism.

Under Alexander II a period of reform and liberalism was introduced and the Jews were allowed a large measure of freedom.

But immediately after his assassination in 1881, a period of extreme reaction set in. Pogroms were the usual lot of the Russian Jew and so intolerable was the position that large numbers left Russia to seek new homes in Britain or America, while others began to think of a return to Palestine.

The Haskalah

During the latter half of the 19th century, Russian Jewry witnessed the emergence of a new philosophy of enlightenment which embraced European culture with as much ardour as previous generations had repudiated it. The new movement originated in Germany and quickly spread to the other great centres of Jewish life. Young Talmud students began to take up the study of European culture and also to introduce a scientific approach to Jewish subjects.

The Haskalah did much to introduce a pure spoken Hebrew, and also to set in motion a powerful current of creative Yiddish literature.

Two main streams flowed from the Haskalah movement: the assimilationist and the nationalist.

CHAPTER SEVEN

The Age of Emancipation
1700—1900

Even before the French Revolution broke down the walls of the ghetto, the Jews of Germany were already picking away at them from within. Moses Mendelssohn was one of the foremost leaders of enlightenment and he worked for the emancipation of his people by attempting to introduce them to European culture.

When the cry of Liberty and Equality resounded throughout Europe, the Jews were granted equality of rights in countries overrun by Napoleon. In many cases they began early to pay the price of emancipation by complete assimilation and large numbers of Jews particularly in Germany found their way to the baptismal font. Among those were members of the family of Moses Mendelssohn and the great poet Heine.

Despite the severe reactions of 1815 and 1848 the Jews in Central Europe slowly but surely made their way into public life. In all countries—England, France, Germany—the ghetto walls were trampled down by a stream of Jews who entered occupations and professions which had hitherto been denied to them. Numerous are the names of illustrious Jews in all communities who rose to positions of great eminence as statesmen, scientists, musicians and philanthropists.

Parallel with this was the emergence of Reform Judaism which had its birth in Germany but has proved a power of great importance in America. Into this latter country Jews had arrived with the very earliest settlers. By 1914 there were over 2 million Jews resident in the United States, and in all spheres of American life the Jew has been among the progressive pioneers.

Towards the end of the 19th century it became clear, however, that emancipation had not solved the Jewish question. Political anti-semitism raised its head in Europe and the German Bismarck made the politically progressive Jew his main object of attack. An example of the new antisemitism showed itself in the trial of the French Jew, Alfred Dreyfus. It was during this trial that Theodore Herzl clearly recognised the crux of the Jewish problem. His "Jewish State" was the result. With the first Zionist Congress of 1897 and the launching of the Zionist movement began the most hopeful development in Jewish life. Zionism seemed the one answer to the two-fold problem of assimilation and attack which had faced the Jew wherever he lived.

CHAPTER EIGHT

The Jews in Our Own Day

The Early Struggles of Zionism

Some years before Herzl, many writers and thinkers such as Lillienblum, Kalischer, Hess, Pinsker and Smolenskin had advocated that the salvation of the Jew lies in his return to Palestine. The Chovevei Zion movement had taken modest preliminary steps to further this aim. Herzl approached his task in a much more ambitious and urgent frame of mind. He spent himself in the attempt to secure an official charter which would secure Palestine as a Jewish State. After his death, his successors continued the struggle. In the meantime, new Jewish settlements, villages and towns were built in Palestine, the Hebrew language was revived and the Jewish spirit began to breath freely once again in its ancient homeland.

The Growth of Zionism

The Balfour Declaration of 1917 added a new impetus to the Jewish longing to rebuild the country. The successive aliyoth brought many thousands of immigrants who set themselves the task of creating the miracle of a country transformed. Side by side with this the Arab opposition grew, which led to increasing and more complicated difficulties.

The Years 1914-1945

The first World War brought renewed suffering to the Jews of Eastern Europe. In Russia it was natural that many Jews should work for the revolutionary party. On the other hand, many thousands who could not become absorbed in the new State fled from Eastern Europe to America, Canada, Argentine and Brazil.

Other countries were obliged after the first World War to adopt minority treaties granting ordinary rights to minority populations. In effect this was ignored, and the social and economic position of the Jews remained as low as before.

In Germany between the Wars, the opponents of the democratic regime adopted an antisemitic platform and demanded that Germany should be free from its Jews altogether. The National-Socialist Party under Adolf Hitler adopted the massacre of the Jews as its declared policy. In other parts of the world—England and America—the Jews were comparatively free from any violence although from time to time antisemitism in different guises remained a potential source of danger.

The catastrophe which overcame European Jewry in the Second World War of 1939-1945 is unparalleled in the history of any other nation. With six million Jews done to death, over one third of the world Jewish population perished, and among them were the best elements of Jewish life.

The Birth of the Jewish State

The end of the Second World War saw the Jews more than ever determined to establish a Jewish State in Palestine. The insurmountable difficulties of the Jewish-Arab conflict were earnestly discussed by the United Nations who finally agreed in November, 1947, that the country be divided into two separate states. Some months afterwards, Great Britain relinquished her mandate over the country and in May, 1948, the Jews declared an independent State of Israel in its part of the country. The Arab States immediately attacked but the Jews held firm and successfully withstood the powerful opposition of the surrounding Arab States. Within the first ten years of its existence as an independent state Israel had more than doubled her Jewish population by mass immigration of Jews from communities all over the world. By 1961 there were considerably over two million Jews in Israel and in spite of the many political and economic problems which face her, Israel is recognised by Jews all over the world as the greatest source of hope for a creative and happy Jewish people.

AN OUTLINE OF BASIC JUDAISM

XVII

CHAPTER ONE

Judaism—A Definition

1. Difficulty of the Present Task

In many respects this part of the book has been the most difficult part to write. The reason for this is that up to now we have dealt with facts and now we have to deal with ideas. Up to now we have concerned ourselves with the facts of Jewish observance, with the facts of Jewish literary sources and with the facts of Jewish history. Now however we must attempt to understand something of the teachings, ideas and beliefs of Judaism which underline all those facts. And it is not going to be easy because where we can describe a law or custom in one line we would need a book to examine the religious idea which is basic to that law.

2. Deed and Creed

It might be asked why wasn't the present chapter put at the beginning? Surely it would have been more logical to give an account of Jewish beliefs and teachings before dealing with the observances. We may as well admit straight away that it would indeed have been more logical to adopt such a procedure. Yet there is a valid reason for our following the present arrangement. It is because Judaism expresses itself more powerfully and clearly in the **behaviour pattern** of the Jew rather than in his **theology.** Put in another, more popular, way we can say that Judaism rests on **deed** rather than on **creed.** As a matter of fact there has been a silent debate going on among Jewish scholars for a very long time as to whether or not Judaism has any dogmas at all. The dictionary explains a dogma as a settled opinion, a principle or tenet, a doctrine laid down with authority. Some famous Jewish teachers have denied that Judaism can lay claim to any dogma except the belief in the only One God. Others have tried to establish a case for the opposite view by showing how Bible, Talmud and medieval philosophy have upheld a number of beliefs as absolutely basic and so essential to Judaism that a Jew who does not believe in them must be considered an heretic. Perhaps the greater truth lies somewhere between these two extremes. But we are anticipating just a little and perhaps we should first clear a little more ground.

3.   Judaism is not just Religion

When the average person speaks about Judaism he usually means to talk of the Religion of the Jew. But it would be a mistake to think that Judaism and the Jewish Religion are exactly the same thing.

The fact is that the Jewish Religion is only a part—the most important part—of Judaism and we should understand that the term Judaism really connotes much else in addition to the Religion.

Properly understood Judaism is the all-embracing term used to connote the totality of Jewish life and thought. Without any doubt, the Religion of the Jews is the most important single element in Judaism and the one that gives direction to all else. But a proper interpretation of Judaism will show that Jewish literature is also part of Judaism, Jewish history is part of Judaism, Jewish social life is part of Judaism. In brief, there is not a single expression of our age-long life and thought, whether purely religious or secular, political, social or artistic which is not included in the all embracing term—Judaism.

4.   Judaism a Religious Civilisation

This then is the complete meaning of Judaism—not only the Religion, but the Religion and the language, the history and the music, the literature and the politics, the Synagogue and the society—it is all Judaism. But remember, as we look upon this four thousand year old pattern of life we can discern that the characteristic element in this amazingly colourful design is in fact our Religion, that is, the religious law and the religious teaching. Our history is thus characterised by a religious purpose which runs right through it from the earliest beginnings of the Hebrew tribe till the latest development in modern Israel. Again, a distinct religious thread is interwoven throughout our Jewish literature and social life. Even the language of Judaism, Hebrew, has for long been designated as Lashon Hakodesh—"The Holy Tongue". It would therefore be true to say that the Jewish Religion is present in every part of Jewish life and thought to influence it, and often to shape it. In Judaism there is really no division of life into different compartments of secular and religious, for everything permissable in life is touched with Religion just as the Bible and the Talmud deal with all kinds of subjects in addition to the purely religious. Open the pages of the Bible and you find laws of hygiene, agriculture and civil administration. Turn to the Talmud and you find some science, philosophy and history. All subjects belonging to the good way of life find their place inside Judaism with a distinct religious colouring. That is why some writers like to describe Judaism as a religious civilisation. That is why Judaism is so much concerned as a practical way of life with laws and observances. That is why Judaism has produced so many prophets and teachers whose chief aim was to raise the standards of social justice and day to day righteousness among men. That is why, as we had to explain before, Judaism stresses the importance of good deed rather than correct creed.

5. Three Fundamentals

Let us now come back to our description of the Jewish Religion and return to an earlier question. Are there no unique beliefs in the Jewish Religion which distinguish it from all other faiths? The answer we give is, yes. There are indeed unique beliefs characteristic of Judaism. How many there are and whether they can be described as fast dogma which allow no room for interpretation or modification is a matter which the interested student of theology must discover from some of the excellent books which are listed in the bibliography. For our simple purpose however we shall rely on the authority of some of our great sages who have taught us that Judaism is unique in three chief respects which are our belief in God, in Israel and in Torah. We shall take them in that order particularly as it seems the most logical.

CHAPTER TWO

The Jewish Teaching About God

1. The Way of Simple Faith

The Bible begins with the words "In the Beginning God created . . ." In itself this grand opening is significant because it indicates at the very first step that in Judaism the existence of God is a truth which is accepted without prior examination or discussion. "In the beginning God . . . " and generally speaking this has never been doubted by the Jew who has been able to take God's existence for granted. It is sometimes said that the Jew came to his belief in God by intuition, not through reason. That is to say that he possesses his unquestioned faith in God because he has always **felt** that God exists. It is possible, for example, for two people to know that five plus five equal ten. One knows the truth of this proposition as a result of a process of reasoning and philosophical examination while the second knows the truth because he has always felt and believed its truth with an unquestioned faith. In the same way there are two possible ways to our belief in God, the way of reason and the way of simple unquestioned faith. In general, Jews have shown that their approach to a belief in God has been of the second kind.

2. The Way of Reason

However, in common with thinkers of other faiths Jewish scholars at times tried to find proofs for the existence of God. This happened particularly during the Middle Ages. When we look at all these attempted proofs we find that they fall under two chief headings.

First there is the argument from the design of Nature. When we look at the intricacies of life from the wonderfully complicated organism of man down to the animal and plant world we realise that only a master mind could have planned and created this miraculous world and all that is in it. To think that it all came without the creative design and power of God is as unreasonable—more so in fact—as the foolish belief that the printed words on this page all got there by chance or of their own accord. Secondly, there is the argument from experience. That is to say, that in the lives of individuals there is often the feeling of a great but mysterious power that upholds them, gives them ideas of truth and goodness and which moves them to acts of courage or sacrifice. This can apply too in the history of entire nations and in the fact that only that which is good remains stable while evil and wickedness are ultimately destroyed or destroy themselves.

In addition to the above two main arguments, both of which can be divided into many sub-headings, there is the argument from Tradition. This rests entirely on the record found in the Bible of how God created the Universe and revealed himself to Israel giving them the Torah. It also rests on the statements dealing with miracles and no God's intervention in human affairs.

3. One God

Having affirmed the existence of God, Judaism really lays down only one basic idea about Him which is a recognised dogma—the

Unity of God. "Hear O Israel the Lord our God the Lord is One."

This is immediately a negation of the polytheism of the ancient world with its numerous deities. It is a repudiation of the idea that there are two gods or two creative sources of existence, one of good and the other of evil. It is also a clear denial of the idea of a trinity—three gods in One which is the established doctrine of Christianity. For Judaism there can be absolutely no compromise at all in this fundamental concept of the Only One God who is the ultimate creative source of all life and death, the elements of nature and history and the power behind all forces, physical and spiritual.

4. God is the Creator

The Universe and all things in it owes its existence to the creative act of God. At first there was nothing, then from this state of non existence God created the Universe. We cannot argue that it is impossible to create something out of nothing since this presumes to ascribe ordinary human limitations to an All-Powerful and Omnipotent God.

5. God is a Personal God

But God did not create the Universe and then withdraw from it allowing it and all life to proceed along in accordance with the natural laws which He implanted in all things from the beginning. The ancient Greek philosophers also had a conception of God but to them He was simply the First Cause of existence—nothing else. In Judaism, God is concerned in the affairs of man and intervenes in the history of nations and of individuals. He is the "God of Abraham, the God of Isaac and the God of Jacob." No conception of God which separates Him from us would be adequate, and the whole emphasis of Judaism is, therefore, on this "personal" relationship of God with the world which He created. Our God then, is a God who knows us and it is this knowledge which God has of us which gives Religion its whole meaning and which gives the religious man his sense of security. It provides us also with the knowledge and hope that in the final analysis of the history of individuals as well as of nations the justice of a God who knows and who cares must prevail.

6. Anthropomorphism in the Bible

The first word in the above subheading seems rather long and difficult. It means the representation of God in human form. Thus when the Bible speaks of "the finger of God" or of His hand, throne or footstool it uses an anthropomorphism, i.e., a figure of speech to describe a particular aspect of God's nature. Instead of speaking of God's redemptive power in bringing Israel out of Egyptian slavery the Bible poetically writes about God's "outstretched hand." But of course God has no body nor can any physical attributes properly be ascribed to Him. Jewish teachers emphasise God is a great Spirit—no body, no matter. Yet how else could the Bible really make us understand God except by using metaphors which, though simple and naive, at least bring us nearer to Him? We find it easier to understand the power of God if we are given a picture of His powerful outstretched arms. We find it easier to think on the permanent control God exercises over life when we refer to the eye of God resting upon all His creatures.

Here again we have an indication of the personal approach to God by which we bring Him nearer to us and ourselves nearer to Him.

CHAPTER THREE

Israel

1. The Chosen Race

Every day we thank God in our prayers for choosing us from all the other nations. When one is called up to the Reading of the Law the formula of the first blessing is "Blessed art Thou, O Lord our God, King of the Universe, Who has chosen us from all other nations and given us His Torah." The Kiddush and Havdalah for Sabbath and festivals contain sentences with similar ideas. And not only the Prayer Book but also the Bible emphasises again and again this point of the election or the choice of Israel. For reasons of simplification of treatment we are avoiding quotations of texts but if we had to collect here most of the texts in our Prayer Book and Bible which teach this doctrine then we should take up a great deal of space indeed. Now should we examine all these texts we would see quite clearly what this belief implies. It means that God chose Israel for a particular purpose in history.

2. Some Difficulties and their Answers

This doctrine has sometimes presented great difficulties.

(*a*) **Why should God have to choose a people for any particular purpose?** We can perhaps understand the answer to this question when we remember that God constantly uses all sorts of agencies to carry out His will. God uses the wind, fire, the waters—all the elements of the Universe for His special purposes at any time. If you remember what we said before about the "personal" God you will understand that God does not withdraw Himself from history. He is not the God of the distant heavens only but the God of the earth too and all people in it. This means that He can choose individuals for a special mission—as in fact happened in the case of Moses and the prophets. On the face of it therefore there seems nothing impossible in the belief that an entire people—the people of Israel—was chosen by God to perform a particular task on the field of world history.

(*b*) **What is this special purpose?** The answer is clear, it is a religious purpose. To teach the world the truth about the Only One God and the brotherhood of all men. Moreover it is to live a life of highest ethical content in accordance with God's revealed will. Through such a mission, Israel becomes the religious teacher of mankind.

(*c*) **Does not this doctrine of a Divine choice of Israel imply the strange and untenable belief that God favours one section of mankind over another?** To this the answer is a distinct—No. The election of Israel gives no advantage to the Jews; it imposes only extra responsibility. The prophets make this clear again and again. It is because of their special relation to God that Israel has the extra responsibility to live in accord with the moral law.

(*d*) **Why is Israel chosen and not other nations?** The answer to this is found in the Biblical story. The early Hebrews, our ancestors, were the first to blaze the path to a new Religion founded on the truth of the Unity of God. This new found truth established and maintained by Abraham, Isaac and Jacob, became the central fact in Jewish life and ideas. It kept them apart from all others and they disciplined themselves in a way of life that made them religiously and spiritually sensitive. As individuals differ in their abilities and vocations, so the Jews, from the earliest days of their history as a people, showed a special genius for religion. We hold it as a fact of history that ethical monotheism—the belief in and the worship of the One God—was the Jewish contribution to civilisation. The whole course of our history, the complete development of our law and literature has recognised God as the chief motive, as the driving force, as the sole source of inspiration. It is not that we claimed a greater portion of God's cae—more than any other nation. Not at all! It is simply that we, more than any other nation, paid more attention to God and to the Divine and universal ethic of human brotherhood.

There is a remarkable and very illuminating Midrash which tells that before God gave Israel the Law on Mount Sinai, He approached the other nations and offered it first to them—but each in turn refused it because the high ethics and moral responsibility which the Torah taught were too much for them and they refused to be persuaded to live up to such high standards. It was only then that God offered it to Israel who immediately accepted it proclaiming "Naaseh Venishmah" —We shall perform its laws and accept all its teachings. With thi' parable the Rabbis meant to teach that in reality **All Nations** had the opportunity to develop as Israel did. But they never did. The election of Israel may thus be regarded as an historic fact as well as a religious truth.

3. The B'rit or Covenant

This special relationship of Israel to God is expressed by the Hebrew term B'rit or Covenant—one of the key words in Jewish theology. We might use the much simpler term "contract" for our elementary purpose (but bear in mind that there may be objections in comparing the B'rit to a legal contract). The terms of the B'rit are all clearly pu in the document which is the Torah. Here we see that God at a particular point in history, chose Israel for a religious purpose. He established a covenant with them and gave them a Torah to guide their lives. The B'rit represents a permanent relationship that can never be broken. A child born of Jewish parentage is always a member of the covenanted people, just as a son is always a child of his parents. He may be loyal or disloyal to the Covenant—that is really his life's choice—but whatever he does he is still a Jew bound by the mystical obligations of the B'rit.

4. The Pious of other Nations

The belief in the election of Israel, as we have seen, brings Israel no extra advantages but only extra responsibilities. We must now clear up another point in the same discussion. It is that God's reward is not reserved only for the good Jew but is promised to the righteous of all nations. Here is another instance of the uniqueness of Judaism which teaches that God's love is extended to all His creatures Jew and gentile. In Judaism there is no monopoly of salvation to those who possess a cetain faith. We reject such exclusiveness and our teachers have declared that the righteous of all nations have a reward in the world to come.

5. Other Religions

To the Jew, Judaism is the true Faith. But we hold that other religions such as Christianity and Mohammedanism possess partial truth according to the degree to which they approximate to Judaism. The hope of Judaism however is not bound up with the idea that all mankind will become Jews and observe the Law. Our hope is rather centred in the idea that the truth of the One God and the brotherhood of Man will be realised by all mankind and become the guiding force in the practical life of all. To that extent then, the Jew as a son of the ancient Covenant is obliged to sanctify his life and dedicate himself to the universal ideal. He is a member of a particular people with a peculiar charge which he is to carry out for the ultimate good of the whole world. Of course any non-Jew can become a son of the Covenant; but the tests are severe, and rightly so. For very valid historical and social reasons Jews do not actively proselytise non-Jews and the rule today ensures that an intending convert must prove his earnestness and constancy.

6. The God Choosing People

If the doctrine in the election of Israel is to have meaning today it must imply that not only has God chosen Israel but Israel has chosen God. This is our constant obligation under the B'rit made between God and Israel.

In the past, the Jews have shown themselves prepared to sanctify the name of God by remaining loyal to their faith in Him whatever the sacrifice. Persecution and exile made little difference to their steadfastness. If anything, it was strengthened through such trial and because of their loyalty they continued to be unique— a people set apart—whose distinctive outlook, beliefs, practices, religious law and literature gave them continued opportunity of preserving religious truth.

And so even the modern Jew with his modern philosophy of history can, aye, he must still be able to, declare with a perfect faith that from of old his people showed a distinguishing propensity for religious truth. God then elected them and established a B'rit with them by which the Jews became the Divine instrument for spreading a religious

message to all mankind. To enable them to do this the Jews had to
carry out their obligations under the Covenant. They became more
and more a God-choosing people and accepted the responsibility for
the Torah. They brought the belief in God to other peoples and other
faiths and continued ever afterwards to develop through their Torah
their own distinctive God-centred way of life. In all this they **were**
different. But it was difference with a meaning—a religious meaning—
which constantly turned their attention to God who was the central
point of their whole history. Holding firm to their distinguishing
religious way of life, their whole history assumed meaning. Their
sufferings and struggles were of some purpose, because they strove as
a separate people determined to hold on to its own sanctifying religious
way of life—a religious way of life which was intended to act as a
constant guide and inspiration to mankind.

7.   The Particular and the Universal

Running through all the above sections there are two elements
which appear to oppose each other—the particular and the universal.
On the one side we maintain that the Jews are a special people. Separate
from mankind in religious beliefs, practices and vocation: on the other
hand we say that Judaism holds the ideal of the universal brotherhood
of man and that it is a faith that preaches God's salvation to the righteous of all nations and creeds. How do we reconcile these two opposing
ideas? The fact is that they are not really opposing ideas at all. Everyone
recognises that the individual is a member of his family as well as of
the community. In the first he develops his full personality and realises
his individual happiness, growing up in body and in mind to enable
him all the better to take his proper place in the wider community.
There is no antithesis between the family unit and society. In the same
way a Jew is first a member of his own people with their distinctive
laws, customs and culture. In this community he develops to his full
religious potentiality and is then best fitted to play his part as a member
of the wider brotherhood of men. In Judaism there is room for both
particularism and universalism for we don't see them as rivals at all.
Read the two paragraphs of the **Alenu** (S.P.B. p. 76). The first is
particularistic; the second expresses a universal ideal. What we show
in this single prayer can be illustrated in numerous other passages in
the daily Prayer Book, the Festival liturgy and of course in the Bible.
We may summarise it in this way. Judaism is the special religion of a

separate people but the people and the faith are dedicated to the most comprehensive and universal ideals.

CHAPTER FOUR

The Torah and Jewish Law

1. Torah—the Plan for Living

Having dealt first with our belief in God and secondly with our belief in Israel as the distinctive nation which throughout its history has embraced the special vocation of proclaiming God to the world, we must now examine the particular design or pattern by which the Jews have planned their life. This plan for Jewish living is derived from the teaching of the Torah and we shall now briefly examine our belief with regard to the Torah.

2. What is Torah?

First of all, just a few words of explanation about the term itself. In its narrowest meaning Torah refers only to the first five books of Moses—the Pentateuch, from Genesis to Deuteronomy—which is read in sections during the Sabbath morning services in the Synagogue. But quite clearly this is the term which is used also to refer to the whole of the Bible—the Pentateuch, the Prophets and the Writings—all the twenty four books which form the contents of the Old Testament Scriptures, sometimes referred to by its Hebrew term "Tenach"— the initials of the three constituent parts which go to make up the Bible. But if we narrow down the meaning of the word Torah to refer only to our Bible then we wrongly restrict its meaning. Simply put, we can say that **Torah represents the whole Jewish teaching from the commencement of the Bible right down to our own day.** This it seems is the only satisfactory way in which we can truly understand and fully appreciate the essence of this all embracing term Torah.

3. The Written Law

We are taught to think of two kinds of Torah. One representing what is called the "Torah she-bichtav" or the written Torah, and the other called "Torah she-beal peh" or the oral tradition of the Torah.

Let us deal first with the written Torah. This is, as we have already explained, the Bible, and forms the fundamental essence of Jewish

teaching on which all else is built. The distinguishing point about the
Bible or the written Torah is that its teachings and values are intended
as permanent.

4. The Law and Revelation

The most important part of the Written Law is the Pentateuch and
this is regarded as revealed i.e. the outcome of a special Revelation of
God to Moses and the people. Our sages and teachers have never ex-
hausted this fundamental theme but ultimately it is a doctrine we
accept on faith. At the same time it is not a blind faith but essentially
reasonable. For surely God would no more leave us to our own design
than a parent would abandon his beloved child leaving him to his own
whims. God's plan for the perfection of man needs an instrument to
enable man to achieve his ultimate spiritual goal. That instrument God
gave in the form of Divine Law which He revealed to Moses and the
people of Israel. The 19th and 20th chapters of Exodus give us an
account of God's revelation on Sinai to proclaim the commandments.
How God spoke and how the people heard is something which must
always remain the greatest mystery of religious teaching. The essential
doctrine which we must stress here however is that the laws of the
Pentateuch are not man made but are from God who ordained them,
in a manner not fully understood by us, for the purpose of enabling
man to reach a state of spiritual perfection.

5. The Rest of the Bible

Much of the remaining parts of the Bible are the historical records of
the people of Israel from the time they entered Canaan until shortly
after the destruction of the First Temple less than one thousand years
later. But interspersed in the history we have the teachings of the
prophets and we read how these great men had visions of God and
communed with Him. In a very real sense this too is a revelation of
God to his chosen spirits. The Hebrew prophet is thus God inspired
and whenever he speaks to the people he never does so in his own name
but always in the name of God. "Thus saith the Lord" is ever the
tremendous introduction to the speeches of the prophets.

It is always God's law and teaching, not their own, which they
transmit to the people. These prophets, and there have been none like
them since, were as close to the spirit of God as it is possible for a
human mind to imagine and their teachings are consequently spoken
of as a revelation from God.

This then is the Torah she-bichtav, the Written Law—representing in Jewish belief the basic and permanent values of the Jewish religious civilisation. From it we derive our early historical narratives, from it also we derive the fundamental ethics of Judaism and from this written Torah we derive our laws and traditions governing the Jewish observances of Sabbath and festivals, the dietary laws and the various ritual practices which form so essential a part of Jewish religious life.

6. The Law and Development

Now while recognising that the basic laws and ethical teachings of the Written Law are permanent and valid for all time, it is obvious that each age is faced with different conditions of life arising out of the ever changing circumstances. With each successive generation new ideas and different values are created, caused by the continuous development of human life and thought. The changing historical and economic scene makes it impossible for us to hold firm to the concept of a law which shall be changeless in all its details. It is sometimes supposed that Jewish religious law is chained down to the past and has no relevance to modern Jewish life which has moved irrevocably on to leave the old law forlorn and unheeded. Nothing could be further from the truth, and here it becomes necessary for us to understand the full meaning of what we called our second Torah, Torah she-beal peh, the Oral Law or the Oral tradition.

7. The Oral Law

From the moment the books of the Bible became available they formed the basis of exposition, explanation and interpretation. The Bible was rarely, if ever, taken in its simple literal meaning. On the contrary, it was the ever present text for ceaseless interpretation. To emphasise this point the Rabbis explained that together with the Written Code divinely revealed to Moses, he also received oral explanation. These oral explanations were handed down to Joshua, his successor, who passed them on to the prophets from whom it went to the elders—all the time going through a continuous process of development until they were finally handed on to the rabbis who were the true successors to the prophets. It must be kept clearly in mind that the Oral Law forms an integral part of the Torah since without it much of the significance of Biblical laws would be lost. The example of Tephilin is clear and well known. The Bible simply states "And thou shalt bind them for a sign upon thy hand and they shall be for frontlets between thine eyes." There is nothing here to indicate how this command is to be carried out in practice. How then do we know? Only from the Oral Law and tradition. What applies to Tephilin can be said of all other laws in the Bible.

It is of some interest and of no little importance for us to note that this body of Oral Law was not at first written down in any authoritative code, the reason being that whereas the principles of Biblical Law were written down as unaltered, the Oral Law and tradition were meant to be anything but permanent. Quite clearly they were intended to express themselves in different forms in accordance with the ideas of successive ages. The Oral Law was then the ever changing expression of the standards and attitudes of different generations of Jewish teachers. It was only after the destruction of the Temple in the 1st century when it was feared that Jewish religious life was on the point of disintegration that the rabbis set about the task of collecting the mass of oral laws and traditions of the Jewish people. When this was finally done and edited in the collection known as the Mishnah it did not necessarily put a stop to the development of Jewish Oral Law for after that came the Gemara which represents the development of the Oral Law for the next 300 years. To some it might seem that the abnormal historical conditions of the Jewish people stultified any further development, and while there may be some truth in that, it is by no means the whole or even more than a very small part of the truth for the fact is that even after the completion of the Talmud this development is taking place and no doubt the more normal Jewish life in Israel will result in a strengthening of this process.

8. The Torah as a Developing Law

The essential point to note from all this is that while the Bible is changeless, interpretation and rabbinical tradition is meant to be changed and adapted by us as the natural national expression of our age. Those who become restless with Jewish tradition must beware lest in their enthusiasm for development they do not support revolution against the whole authority of the very fundamentals of Jewish law and the abrogation and destruction of the Bible as the Jewish charter. There is an essential difference between development and revolution, between Judaism and another creed. This is often the difference between Orthodox and Liberal Judaism.

On the other hand we would do well to remember that the rabbis of old were great realists who adapted the oral tradition to serve their own age and so managed to keep their people within the discipline of Torah. To cavil at every development is as unrealistic as it is in fact untraditional.

The traditional teachings of the Jewish people make it clear that we are to believe with a perfect faith that our Bible is a Divinely revealed body of religious practices and moral law which we accept as the basic pattern for Jewish life. We further hold that our religious teachers and leaders have been responsible for the development of the interpretations and traditions of the Jewish religious civilisation, all of which are based on the Bible and that this body of rabbinic tradition is capable of ordered and systematic development from age to age in accordance with the reason and conscience of the Jewish people.

CHAPTER FIVE

The Messiah

1. A Principle of Our Faith

Having dealt with the three basic concepts of Judaism—God, Israel, and Torah, we shall now deal briefly with several other ideas of Judaism which hold a central position in our Faith. The first of these is our belief in the Messiah.

One of the final principles of the Jewish Faith as enumerated by the great medieval Jewish thinker, Maimonides, reads as follows: "I believe with a perfect faith in the coming of the Messiah, and, though he tarry, I will wait daily for his coming."

2. The Meaning of the Term

The Hebrew word for Messiah—Mashiach, means literally "anointed" and was the term often used of a Jewish King or of a High Priest both of whom were anointed with oil as part of their ceremony of induction. The term thus came to signify one who was specially chosen from among his people for a particular destiny. In this sense the King was the Mashiach or anointed one and so was the High Priest.

This too is the term which Judaism applied to the personality who would, with God's inspiration and through God's power, redeem Israel and inaugurate on earth a wonderful new period of happiness for all mankind. The Messiah is thus in the real meaning of the word anointed and appointed by God.

3. The Work of the Messiah

What would be the tasks of the Messiah? Generally speaking, his coming would accomplish three things which would reflect on the life of (*a*) the individual, (*b*) the People of Israel, (*c*) all mankind.

With regard to the first, all suffering would cease, the righteous vindicated and rewarded, while the wicked would be justly punished.

With respect to the second accomplishment, Israel the suffering nation, would be gathered in from the four corners of exile and re-established in its ancient land. Finally, a period of peace and happiness would be inaugurated for all men who would then acknowledge the sovereignty of the One God.

4. The Prophets' Vision of the Messiah

The Mashiach or Messiah had for the prophets a clearly outlined form. He would be a descendant of the house of David who was King according to God's will and from whom there radiates all the brilliant and great memories of the people and their religion. This Messiah would be a man of flesh and blood, a real personal Messiah. The prophet Isaiah visualises him as follows: "And there shall come forth a shoot out of the stock of Jesse and a branch out of his roots shall bear fruit; and the spirit of the Lord shall rest upon him, the spirit of wisdom and understanding, the spirit of counsel and might, the spirit of knowledge and the fear of the Lord; and his delight shall be in the fear of the Lord; and he shall not judge after the sight of eyes, neither reprove after the hearing of his ears, but with righteousness shall he judge the poor, and reprove with equity for the meek of the earth; and he shall smite the earth with the rod of his mouth, and with the breath of his lips shall he slay the wicked. And righteousness shall be the girdle of his loins, and faithfulness the girdle of his reins."

5. Belief in a Personal Messiah

Such was the pattern of this ideal man—the Mashiach, the anointed of God about whom the early prophets spoke with such rapture. But it must be clearly noted that the Messiah is no supernatural being and certainly not divine. Such a concept would militate against all that is sacred and basic in Judaism. Wherever the figure of a personal Messiah is portrayed in Judaism it is of a man who has been imbued with special inspiration by God to carry out God's message on earth.

6. The Messianic Hope in Jewish History

The Messianic Hope remained very much in the forefront of Jewish consciousness to inspire and encourage and to comfort. In times of darkest need when the heavy clouds of persecution enveloped the Jewish people, when oppression and massacre were their only lot in the world this fervent hope in better times, this single simple faith in a Mashiach was the sole ray of light which illumined what was otherwise a world of unrelieved blackness and despair.

In our days when the long lines of Jews were marched off by the Nazis to their death in the crematoria and gas chambers of central and eastern Europe, there yet was heard that wonderful song of hope and faith in the coming of the Messiah. Those courageous men, women and children who faced death with Jewish song on their lips and sang of the Messiah sang of no philosophical interpretation of an ancient dogma of their Faith but sang with fervent hearts of the Divinely appointed Messiah, who would be sent by God to bring an end to their persecution.

7. Belief in the Messianic Age

Side by side, with the belief in a personal Messiah we find in the writings of the prophets and Jewish teachers a Messianic conception which stresses not so much the coming of one particular personality as of an ideal age of peace and good-will brought about through the endeavours of all. The hope is not so much for one man who will renew the world, but for the new world that is to arise afterwards upon the earth. For it is perhaps inconsistent with the way of Judaism that one man should be lifted above humanity to be its destiny. The conception of **one man** retires into the background in favour of the conception of **one time:** the Messiah gives way to the **days of the Messiah**. There is nothing heretical in this view of the Messiah, and, in fact, the one view of the Messiah does not exclude the other. The hope is the same Jewish hope for a redeemed Israel and a redeemed mankind. The difference lies perhaps in the matter of emphasis on the efforts of one man or on the concerted efforts of all men of good will working with the spirit of God as their guiding power. The end however is the same.

8. The Kingdom of God

Bound up in the hope in the Messiah is the forward looking ideal of the Jew who, in the optimism which is part of Judaism, prays for the establishment on earth of the Kingdom of God—Malchut Shaddai. The term "kingdom of God" is not an announcement of something which will descend upon earth from some other world, much less is it the divine pattern in the Life after Death. The kingdom of God is the world of man as it should be in the eyes of God—the ideal world in which all evil will be removed by man in accordance with the teaching of God. It is moreover the ideal world not for the Jew alone but for all nations—and is the highest conception of the universalistic teachings of Judaism. This hope finds its classical expression in the prophecies of Isaiah and Micah—"And it shall come to pass in the end of days that the mountain of the Lord's house shall be established on the top of the mountains, and shall be exalted above the hills, and all nations shall flow unto it. And many peoples shall go and say: 'come ye and let us go up to the mountain of the Lord, to the house of the God of Jacob, and He will teach us of His ways and we will walk in His paths,' for out of Zion will go forth the Law and the word of the Lord from Jerusalem. And He shall judge between nations, and shall decide for many people; and they shall beat their swords into ploughshares, and their spears into pruning hooks; nation shall not lift up sword against nation, neither shall they learn war any more."

9. The Relevance of the Teaching for Our Day

The belief in the Messiah, whether it be in a personal Messiah or in a Messianic Age, is as fundamental to us in our modern world as ever it was in days gone by. It is this Jewish teaching in Messiah which gives Judaism its character of optimism and which must inspire us to achieve national redemption and also that precious goal of universal happiness when the law of God will reign supreme. Towards the preparation for that ideal the Jewish people has played its part in days of old and Jews who remain faithful to this teaching of their ancient Faith have constantly before them an ideal which can fill their days with a practical programme of noble activity, which will help towards building the Kingdom of God on earth.

CHAPTER SIX

Some Other Important Teachings

Before we conclude this survey of the fundamental teachings of the Jewish Religion we ought to say something, however briefly, on the following.

1. Man is Free

Throughout history thinkers of many lands and different ages have debated the problem of man's freedom. The question may be put like this. Is man free to choose good or evil of his own will or does he act in a certain way because he is compelled as a result of circumstances outside his will and over which he has no control? Those compelling circumstances may be his poverty, his ill health, his social position or even the will of God Himself.

People of varying opinions have taken sides in this question. Quite obviously, it is an important question because if we hold that man's conduct is not freely chosen (Free Will) then man cannot be held responsible for his conduct and the good man does not deserve any reward, no more than the wicked man merits any punishment. If such is the truth then moral judgment must break down.

Now in Judaism there can be no doubt about this problem since all our religious sources, the Bible, the Prayer Book, the Talmud, the rabbis and philosophers are unanimous in the matter. They all maintain (despite one or two passages which only appear inconsistent) that man is free to choose whichever path he wishes to follow, either the good or the bad. Even when circumstances are against him it is his duty to rise above them and choose the good. Man is therefore free and he is completely responsible for what path he chooses for himself.

2. Reward and Punishment

The above statement leads us naturally to the Jewish doctrine of Reward and Punishment, known in Jewish literature as **Sachar Va'onesh.** Since man is free and God is just then somehow or other the righteous man will be vindicated and receive his just merits even as the wicked man will be condemned and be punished.

The faith of Judaism is in a moral order which is bound up with God's justice and it is therefore inconceivable that there should not be Reward and Punishment.

Sometimes we see this working itself out in the lives of individuals and nations when we realise that evil destroys the wicked with the certainty of a lethal weapon. Very often we see nothing of the kind. On the contrary the old question of the Psalmist faces us "Why do the wicked prosper" while the righteous man appears to have nothing but suffering for his lot?

This is the great question of Religion—the shadow that occasionally falls across the brightly illumined path of faith. Many and various are the answers that have been suggested: some of them really satisfying answers and it is a pity that in a brief elementary Guide Book like this it would be out of place to deal with this question. It must suffice then for our present purpose to say that ultimately we stand firm in our belief in God's justice. In His way and in His time all men receive their just reward in accordance with their conduct on earth.

3. Sin

Man is born without sin. His soul is pure and although in life temptation may be great and he shows an inclination to sin, Judaism repudiates any idea that he is born with an original sin that is transmitted to him from the first Adam. Man may have the tendency to sin but this is a very different thing from suggesting that he has the destiny to sin. Further, although a man may be sinful by inclination he has within him the power to **rid himself** of sin.

4. Repentance

However evil be the sin of a man Judaism holds out the glorious promise of atonement. To atone for one's sins is the purpose of one of the great festivals in our religious calendar. Atonement must be preceded by a sincere repentance on the part of the sinner who not only regrets his past sins but resolutely determines not to sin again. In the case of a sin against one's fellow man, we are taught that God does not forgive until restitution is made. In Judaism there is of course no intermediary between God and man and every man approaches God directly through prayer.

5. Life after Death

Quite clearly, some form of belief in eternal life is inherent in the nature of the Jewish religion. Man's origin is eternal and even in death this origin is not obliterated. The direction of his life stretches beyond the boundary of earthly existence. Beyond the beginning and beyond the end there is the nearness of God the eternal source and eternal end. Judaism emphasises the spiritual and godlike characteristics in man. The reality of our existence is this spiritual or soul element within us which is exalted above death. Even beyond death our soul life remains life. This is the teaching of Judaism and it is one which brings peace and added meaning to life on earth. The Jewish belief in life after death has throughout the history of Jewish religious thought been incorporated among the cardinal principles of our Faith.

But not only our Faith, our intuition also leads us to a belief in the deathlessness of the soul. The spark of the divine spirit, the **neshamah,** the soul of man is immortal and is not confined within the limitations of time. It belongs to the Infinite and in that sense we can say that it returns to its Divine Creator. The profound intuitive longing of man for a deeper meaning in life and for a sense of worth and permanency finds its expression in this faith.

6. Speculation kept in Check

A great deal of confusion, however, arises as soon as attempts are made to examine the particular form of this life after death. And here Judaism adopted a stand of its own. Speculation and a morbid excess of fancy were kept in check, and true Judaism would discourage efforts to spy out the soul and to find ways of seeing or hearing the spirits of the dead—a tendency which is felt to be as dangerous as the necromancy of the heathens. Having propounded the belief in the deathlessness of the soul the authoritative teaching of Judaism warns us against useless speculation about the details of life after death.

7. The Secret and the Revealed

Our task is not to worry about the mysteries. Our minds are human minds and therefore limited; we can achieve nothing by delving into the impenetrable chambers of the Creator. These things belong to God. To man belong the revealed things relevant to this world and to our daily lives. The duty of man is to recognise the Law of God which is revealed and near to him. This it is important for us to understand— that it is our task to live a good life on **this earth,** and to leave the secrets of the other world to God. Our duty is clear, it is simple, it is revealed.

8. The True concern of the Jew is for the Good Life on Earth

It is perhaps this very aspect of Judaism that accounts for the passion the Jew has always shown for justice and social reform. The Jew is always in the forefront of the battle for freedom and liberty—justice and better conditions of life for his fellow men.

He cannot help being concerned about man's welfare **on earth**; it belongs to the very essence of Judaism and it is precisely because the Jewish soul loved life so abundantly that it could even dare to predict a time when God would annihilate death forever. It is this keen longing for an energetic, full and beautiful life here on earth which has earned for Judaism the description of "the optimistic and cheery creed." Optimistic because our faith stretches on into the impenetrable future in the belief that God has implanted within us immortal life. Cheery, because having graped that essential faith we will not allow our main duty on earth to be diverted into the strange paths of unreal speculation but it teaches us to concentrate all our efforts and energy in conducting ourselves as children of God in this world, here and now.

Bibliography
(Suggested for further study)

Religion

THE JEWISH RELIGION, M. Friedlander, Shapiro, Vallentine, London, (1953)

THE JEWISH FESTIVALS, S. M. Lehrman, Shapiro, Vallentine, London, (1943)

THE ESSENCE OF JUDAISM, L. Baeck, Schocken, New York, (1948)

THE JEWISH WAY OF LIFE, I. Epstein, Goldston, London, (1946)

JUDAISM, I. Epstein, Epworth Press, London, (1945)

THE FAITH OF JUDAISM, I. Epstein, London, (1954)

JUDAISM AS CREED AND LIFE, M. Joseph, Routledge, (1929)

THE JEWISH HERITAGE, ed. E. Levine, Vallentine, Mitchell, London, (1952)

JEWISH PRAYER, L. Jacobs, Jewish Chronicle Publications, London, (1955)

WE HAVE REASON TO BELIEVE, L. Jacobs, Vallentine, Mitchell, (1957)

A GUIDE TO YOM KIPPUR, L. Jacobs, Jewish Chronicle Publications, London, (1957)

A GUIDE TO PASSOVER, I. Levy, Jewish Chronicle Publications, (1958)

A GUIDE TO SUCCOTH, I. Fabricant, Jewish Chronicle Publications, London, (1958)

A GUIDE TO HANUKKAH AND PURIM, S. M. Lehrman, Jewish Chronicle Publications, London, (1958)

A GUIDE TO ROSH HA-SHANAH, L. Jacobs, Jewish Chronicle Publications, (1959)

A GUIDE TO SHAVUOTH, C. Pearl, Jewish Chronicle Publications, London, (1959)

A GUIDE TO THE SABBATH, S. Goldman, Jewish Chronicle Publications, London, (1961)

INTRODUCTION TO JUDAISM, I. Fishman, Vallentine, Mitchell, (1958)

GOD AND MAN IN JUDAISM, L. Baeck, Vallentine, Mitchell, (1958)

Sources of Jewish Life and Thought

THE HOLY SCRIPTURES, J.P.S.A., (1947)

THE PENTATEUCH AND HAFTORAHS, J. H. Hertz, Soncino Press, London, (1947)

THE SONCINO CHUMASH AND BOOKS OF THE BIBLE, A. Cohen, Soncino Press, London, (1945)

Bibliography

AUTHORISED DAILY PRAYER BOOK with Commentary, J. H. Hertz Shapiro, Vallentine, (1947)

THE MISHNAH, H. Danby, Clarendon Press, (1949)

THE SONCINO TALMUD, ed. I. Epstein, Soncino Press, (1929)

THE SONCINO MIDRASH, ed. H. Freedman and M. Simon, Soncino Press, London, (1939)

EVERYMAN'S TALMUD, A. Cohen, Dent, London, (1932)

A HISTORY OF JEWISH LITERATURE, M. Waxman, Bloch, New York, (1942)

Hebrew

GESENIUS HEBREW GRAMMAR, Kautsch, Cowley, Oxford

INTRODUCTORY HEBREW GRAMMAR, Davidson, Edinburgh

HEBREW FOR ALL, H. Levy, Central Council for Jewish Education, (1950)

A NEW HEBREW GRAMMAR, Fundaminsky, London, (1955)

History

Lady Magnus', OUTLINES OF JEWISH HISTORY, (Revised), Vallentine, Mitchell, London, (1958)

HISTORY OF OUR PEOPLE IN BIBLE TIMES, J. Halpern, Shapiro, Vallentine, London, (1948)

HISTORY OF OUR PEOPLE IN RABBINIC TIMES, J. Halpern, Shapiro, Vallentine, London, (1948)

HISTORY OF THE JEWS, S. Grayzel, J.P.S.A., (1952)

A SHORT HISTORY OF THE JEWS, C. Roth, East and West, London, (1953)

THE FINAL SOLUTION, G. Reitlinger, Vallentine, Mitchell, London, (1953)

JEWISH HISTORY IN PAMPHLETS, C. Pearl and J. Halpern, World Jewish Congress, London

Reference

THE JEWISH ENCYCLOPEDIA, Funk and Wagnall, New York, (1901)

JEWISH YEAR BOOK, Jewish Chronicle, London, Annually

A MINORITY IN BRITAIN, Ed. M. Freedman, Vallentine, Mitchell, London, (1955)

A DICTIONARY OF JUDAISM, R. S. Brookes, Shapiro, Vallentine, London, (1960)

General Index

General Index